ICS   will   £1.99

CONTENTS

D0532879

INTRODUCTION

Although the main mechanical parts of the engine are normally very reliable, problems can arise with oil and coolant leaks. SERVICING YOUR ENGINE AND BRAKES tells you how to deal with them. It also deals with routine valve adjustment and major cylinder head work as well as describing the action to take if your engine suddenly packs up.

The techniques used for setting valve clearances on overhead valve (OHV) and overhead cam (OHC) engines and checking cylinder compression are shown in detail. If there is trouble with the valves or cylinder gasket you will have to remove the cylinder head – this is explained fully, together with instructions on how to decoke and service the head while it is off. The refitting operation is also described, along with adjustments to the timing belt on overhead cam designs.

Trace engine oil leaks and stop them by fitting replacement gaskets and oil seals. Tracking down elusive coolant leaks is also covered and there are instructions on fitting new engine core plugs and replacing the water pump.

Your car relies on effective brakes to bring it safely to a halt. This book gives the low-down on checking and replacing the pads and shoes, and adjusting drum brakes. Leaks in the brake system have to be dealt with at once to avoid failure – learn how to check out the calipers and cylinders and the pipes and hoses. Replacement of major brake components such as drum brake wheel cylinders and the master cylinder is also dealt with and brake bleeding techniques are explained, together with servicing and adjusting the handbrake.

© Eaglemoss Publications Ltd 1988

Based on *Car Care* First Edition © 1985,
Eaglemoss Publications Ltd,
Car Maintenance Course
First Edition © 1983 and *Book of the Car* First Edition © 1970,
Drive Publications Ltd, Berkeley Square House, London W1X 5PD

ISBN 0 86145 702 1

Printed in Great Britain by Severn Valley Press Ltd

Skill level

The jobs in this book are graded by a spanner system according to the level of skill needed:

basic   intermediate   advanced

⚠️ **Warning**

It's all too easy in car maintenance to make a mistake and damage a vital (and often costly) component – or yourself. This symbol highlights possible dangers. Read the accompanying warning carefully so you and your car come to no harm.

☆ **Hints and tips**

This symbol points to inside information or advice – tricks of the trade to make a difficult job easier.

What to do
if the engine packs up

Finding the fault

The faults most likely to stop the car are those that interrupt the fuel supply or sparks. You can check the sparks at the plugs and the fuel supply at the carburettor, but if you find nothing you will have to start checking further back down the systems. This means looking at the fuel pump and the coil and distributor.

If the ignition warning light will not come on, check that the LT wires at the coil are clean and connected and that all the fuses are intact – twist them or clean the ends to make sure they're making contact. Make sure the engine's earth strap is firmly attached.

If the throttle cable has broken, the accelerator pedal will be resting against the floor. You can sometimes transfer the choke cable to the throttle linkage at the carburettor and drive home using the choke control as a hand throttle.

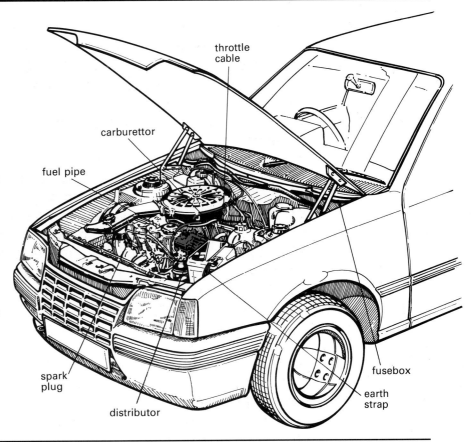

throttle cable

carburettor

fuel pipe

spark plug

distributor

fusebox

earth strap

It's annoying enough being stranded at the roadside when the engine packs up, and matters are made worse if you don't know what the problem is. But it could be that something fairly minor has gone wrong, which you can easily put right when you've found the cause.

Engines usually stop suddenly only if they suffer from a lack of fuel or sparks. An engine that stops dead without prior warning has probably had a sudden ignition failure – although if it locks solid it's more likely to have seized.

A slower, spluttering halt, on the other hand, probably indicates fuel problems – ignition faults that cause similar poor running are unlikely to stop the engine in the short term.

Systems checks

You can make a quick check on whether the ignition system is working by pulling off one of the HT leads at the plug and either resting the metal end connector within ¼in

(6mm) of the engine block, or inserting a spark plug and resting that against the block instead. If you can't do either, insert a piece of metal into the cap and rest that near the engine block. Get a helper to crank the engine over on the starter motor – if the ignition system is working properly, blue sparks will jump the gap.

To check whether the fuel is flowing, disconnect the fuel pipe at the carburettor and see if fuel gushes out when the pump runs. It is best to aim the pipe into an old jar when doing this, but if you can't find one just point the pipe at the ground, keeping it well clear of the hot exhaust pipe and any electric cables. To run an electric pump, all you need to do is get someone to turn on the ignition, but to operate a mechanical one you need to crank the engine over on the starter.

Both types of pump should deliver a strong flow of fuel, normally at the rate of a few squirts of fuel every second.

Permanent stoppage

A more expensive form of engine stoppage is a 'blow up', or mechanical failure.

This usually only happens after a total loss of oil pressure or after extreme overheating, both of which the car's instruments or warning lights will warn you of in time to save the engine by switching it off.

If you don't notice the warnings, loss of oil pressure will manifest itself as a heavy rattling or hammering from the engine. The onset of overheating will announce itself by a very light rattling caused by pinking or pre-ignition.

Fuel problems

Mechanical fuel pumps do not usually fail without warning: more commonly, the fixings loosen off and the pump moves away from the engine slightly so that the pump's lever cannot achieve its full stroke and fuel delivery is greatly reduced.

If the pump is securely mounted but fuel delivery is a problem, you may be able to increase flow by removing some of the gaskets or spacers between it and the engine. Don't remove the thick spacer – this may lead to pump damage.

Electric pumps can suddenly stop working if their contacts become corroded. To check, listen with the ignition on for the pump ticking.

If there are no apparent problems but the car has run more and more badly until it has reached a standstill, remove the fuel filler cap. If there is a sharp rush of air when you do this, the vent is blocked – the pump cannot suck against a significant vacuum. You can get home by driving with the cap loose or by periodically removing the cap to vent the tank.

Check the flexible hoses for leaks and splits. Tighten the hose clips if any have come loose.

Check fuel flow by removing the fuel pipe from the carburettor, and turn the engine over on the starter.

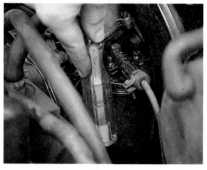
If the float chamber is flooding tap it with a screwdriver handle to reseat the needle valve.

If a mechanical fuel pump has come loose, retighten it removing gaskets or spacers as necessary.

Ignition problems

If the engine stops dead, the chances are that the fuse (if one is fitted) protecting the ignition coil has blown. If the ignition light will not come on but most of the electrics work this is almost certainly the problem. You can substitute a fuse of the correct size from another, less vital component and carry on. But check first that the failure was not caused by a short circuit – a bare connector, for example – and insulate any suspect wires or connections with tape. Check also that the engine's earth strap has not become disconnected or split, as this will give similar symptoms.

In wet weather, a worsening misfire which eventually stops the engine is usually because of damp getting into the ignition components. Dry the HT leads and the inside of the distributor cap thoroughly. If you have any water-resistant spray with you, give the parts a liberal coating once you have reassembled them.

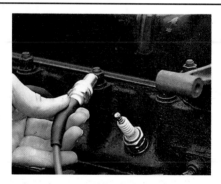
Check for sparks at the plugs using a spare plug in the HT lead. Hold it against the engine block.

Replace a blown coil fuse with another, after checking for shorted out connections.

Make sure the points are opening by removing the distributor cap then rocking the car in gear.

If the ignition system is wet dry off excess water. Spray with water repellent if you have some.

Adjusting the valves on an OHV engine

Overhead valve adjusters

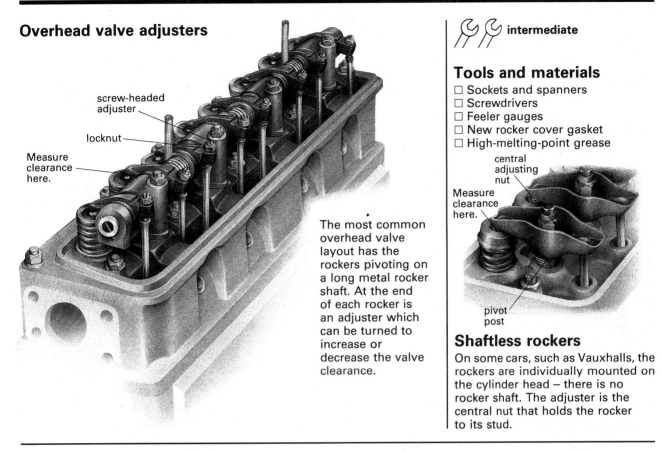

screw-headed adjuster

locknut

Measure clearance here.

The most common overhead valve layout has the rockers pivoting on a long metal rocker shaft. At the end of each rocker is an adjuster which can be turned to increase or decrease the valve clearance.

central adjusting nut

Measure clearance here.

pivot post

Shaftless rockers

On some cars, such as Vauxhalls, the rockers are individually mounted on the cylinder head – there is no rocker shaft. The adjuster is the central nut that holds the rocker to its stud.

intermediate

Tools and materials
☐ Sockets and spanners
☐ Screwdrivers
☐ Feeler gauges
☐ New rocker cover gasket
☐ High-melting-point grease

On an overhead valve (OHV) engine, the valves are operated by the camshaft via rocker arms. When a valve is closed, there is a small gap between its top and the rocker arm. This gap is the valve clearance (commonly called the tappet clearance). It is designed in by the manufacturers to allow for metal expansion as the engine warms up.

The size of the gap is vital to good engine performance – if the gap is too wide, the valves won't open fully and the engine will be noisy. If it is too small, the valve may be held slightly open, allowing gases to leak out and the compression pressure to drop.

The valve clearances should be checked at every service – sooner if the valve gear becomes noisy.

The adjusters

The valve clearance is usually adjusted by a slot-headed adjuster screw fitted to one end of the rocker arm. This screw has a rounded end which sits in the end of the pushrod. By screwing it into or out of the rocker arm, you can adjust the gap between the end of the rocker arm and the valve stem. In some cases the end has a flat-sided adjuster which can be turned with a small spanner or pliers.

On most cars the adjuster screw is locked in position by a locknut. But on some cars, notably Fords, a single bolt-headed screw is used. This type has a self-locking thread – no locknut is needed.

The other type of adjuster you may come across, used on Vauxhalls, has the rocker held down by a central nut (see sideline).

Hot or cold?

Before you start, look in your handbook to find out whether the valves should be adjusted 'hot' or 'cold'. Hot means that the engine must be run up to its normal working temperature and then switched off – you have to work quickly to set the clearances before the engine cools. Cold means that the engine must be absolutely stone cold. This usually means that the engine must not have been run for at least six hours.

When to adjust

The clearances have to be adjusted when the gap between the rocker arm and the valve stem is at its maximum, or you will get a false reading. There are several ways of doing this, depending on your car's engine.

The most common method is the 'rule of nine'. This makes use of the fact that it is easier to judge when a valve is open than when it is closed. With the rule of nine, you can open a particular valve fully, then use the rule to find out which corresponding valve is fully closed. You can then check the clearance of the fully closed valve. For more on the rule of nine, see the next sheet.

The rule of nine works only for cars with non-crossflow engines –

☆ TDC clearances

On a few cars, such as the Chrysler Avenger and Sunbeam, the valve clearances are checked with the piston at top dead centre (TDC) on the firing stroke.

To set the piston at TDC, press your thumb over the spark plug hole and get a friend to turn the engine over. You will feel the pressure building up – when it stops doing it the piston is at TDC. You can now go on to check the valve clearance.

⚠ Rocker covers

When you come to remove the rocker cover you will often find that there is a component such as the air filter in the way. If so you will have to remove it before you can get the rocker cover off.

You may also find that the throttle or choke linkage is attached to the cover. If so, it needs to be disconnected.

those with the inlet and exhaust manifolds on the same side of the engine. Cars with crossflow engines, including many Fords, won't work on this principle. Instead, the valves have to be checked 'on the rock' or 'rocking'. This means that, as one pair of valves on a cylinder (say number 1) are opening, both the valves on number 4 cylinder will be fully closed. You can therefore check the valves on number 4 cylinder.

Before you can get at the valves, you must remove the rocker cover. This is held on either by a series of bolts or screws around the edge of the cover, or by a pair of bolts or screws in the top centre of the cover. The bolts are often a special design and need a special tool to remove them.

Remove all the fixings, then lift the rocker cover off and place it to one side.

Turning the engine

You will have to turn the engine by hand. To make this easier, take out all the spark plugs to relieve the compression pressure in the cylinders.

Fit a spanner on to the nut or bolt of the crankshaft pulley (the big one nearest the bottom of the engine) and turn the engine over in its normal direction of rotation until the valves are in the position for checking. On most cars the engine rotates clockwise, but some engines turn anticlockwise. If you are unsure which way to turn, put the car into fourth gear and, making sure it is not on a slope and cannot run away, release the handbrake and push the car forward. Keep an eye on the crankshaft pulley to see which way it turns.

If you cannot get a spanner on to the crankshaft pulley, you can turn the engine over in other ways – you can try pulling it round on the fan belt, you can try pushing the car in gear, or jacking up one of the driving wheels (leaving the other still on the ground) and turning that wheel to turn the engine.

If the engine is adjusted using the rule of nine, see right for details. If it has to be adjusted with the

Removing the rocker cover

The rocker cover is held to the cylinder head with screws (as here) or with bolts or nuts. These may be around the rim of the cover, or else fitted in the centre top. To gain access, you may need to remove other components such as the air filter and emission control pipes.

With the screws or bolts removed, you can lift off the rocker cover. In many cases you will have to manoeuvre the cover around to clear other components. Once it's off, put the cover to one side on a few sheets of newspaper to avoid oil dripping everywhere.

valves on rock, turn the engine over a few times to watch the valves opening and closing. You will see that there is a point in the cycle when both the valves on each cylinder are open a little – that is, both rocker arms are pushing down slightly, and the valves are 'rocking'. If the valves of number 1 cylinder are rocking, then adjust those on number 4, and vice versa.

Checking clearances

With the valves in the correct position, slide a feeler blade, of the correct size specified in your manual or car handbook, into the gap between the rocker arm and the valve stem. If the gap is correct the gauge will be a tight sliding fit. If it won't go in, or it slips in and out without resistance then the valve clearance needs adjusting.

How you do this, depends on the adjuster. On the screw and locknut

The rule of nine

This gives you an easy way of adjusting the valve clearances. But it only works with four-cylinder non-crossflow engines. Crossflow engines have to be adjusted 'on the rock'.

Number the valves from 1 to 8, working back from the front of the engine. When valve number 8 is fully open (when its rocker arm is fully down) valve number 1 is fully closed and can be adjusted. 8 + 1 = 9: hence the rule of nine. Similarly, when 7 is fully open, 2 is fully closed, and so on.

At the same time as 8 is fully open, another valve, 3, is also fully open. So its corresponding valve, 6, is fully closed and can be adjusted at the same time.

Fully open valve number	Adjust valve number
8	1
3	6
5	4
2	7
6	3
4	5
7	2
1	8

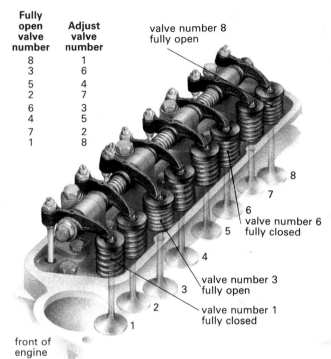

valve number 8 fully open

8
7
6 valve number 6 fully closed
5
4
3 valve number 3 fully open
2
1 valve number 1 fully closed

front of engine

Checking and adjusting the clearances

Slide a feeler gauge blade of the size specified in your handbook, or manual, into the gap between rocker arm and valve stem. If the clearance is right, the feeler should be a tight sliding fit. If it won't go in, or just flaps about then you must adjust the gap.

Using a ring spanner, slacken off the adjuster locknut. Then using a screwdriver in the slot of the adjuster, turn it to increase or decrease the gap as necessary. When the gap is correct, hold the adjuster firm with the screwdriver, and do up the locknut tight.

adjuster, first use a ring spanner to loosen off the locknut. Now use a screwdriver in the slot to adjust the gap with the feeler still in place. Turning clockwise decreases the gap, anticlockwise increases it.

Take care not to tighten down the adjuster too far – you should just feel a slight resistance as you pull the feeler out. Once the clearance appears to be correct, hold the adjusting screw in place with the screwdriver and tighten up the locknut. Recheck the clearance in case it slipped while you were tightening the nut.

Once that valve is done, follow through whichever sequence is appropriate and do all the other valves.

Other adjusters

With the other types of adjuster, the job is a little different. If there is no locknut fitted, then the car has self-locking adjusters. Simply slide in the feeler as before, then turn the bolt to increase or decrease the clearance. There is no need to recheck at the end.

If your engine has shaftless rockers, slide in the feeler and adjust the clearance by moving the central nut. Tightening it reduces the gap, loosening it increases the gap.

Refit the cover

Once all the valves are adjusted, use an old rag to clean the inside of the rocker cover. Carefully clean all traces of old rocker cover gasket from both the cylinder head and the rocker cover with a blunt scraper.

Smear a little high-melting-point grease on to both sides of the gasket then fit it to the rocker cover or the engine block. On some rocker covers there are metal lips fitted which the gasket has to fit inside – make sure it does.

Refit the rocker cover taking care not to trap any wires or cables underneath, then refit all the screws or bolts finger tight. Work evenly around them doing them up half a turn at a time. Tighten the rocker cover down just enough to 'nip' the gasket – no more.

Refit all the cables, pipes, the air filter and anything else you removed. Start the engine and check for oil leaks from the gasket.

Other types of adjuster

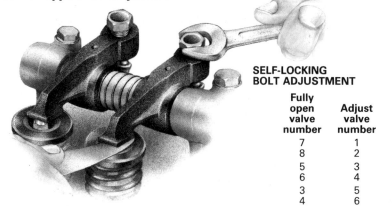

SELF-LOCKING BOLT ADJUSTMENT

Fully open valve number	Adjust valve number
7	1
8	2
5	3
6	4
3	5
4	6
1	7
2	8

On some Ford engines, there is no locking nut for the adjuster (above). Instead you keep the feeler gauge in place while you turn the self-locking bolt.

Most Ford engines are crossflow and don't obey the rule of nine. They have their own pairing between open and closed valves (above right).

SHAFTLESS ROCKER ADJUSTMENT

On cars with a shaftless rocker arm, you adjust the clearance by turning the central nut (right).

Refitting the rocker cover

Before you refit the cover, wipe it clean of dirt and sludge and remove all traces of the old gasket. Fit a new rocker cover gasket, making sure that it aligns with all the bolt holes and is not kinked. Lower the cover on to the cylinder head and refit all the bolts loosely. Tighten them up a little at a time until they just 'nip' the gasket.

Adjusting the valves on an OHC engine

Indirect-acting camshaft

The type of valve layout shown here is mostly used by Ford on their Pinto engine, fitted to the Cortina, Capri and Sierra.

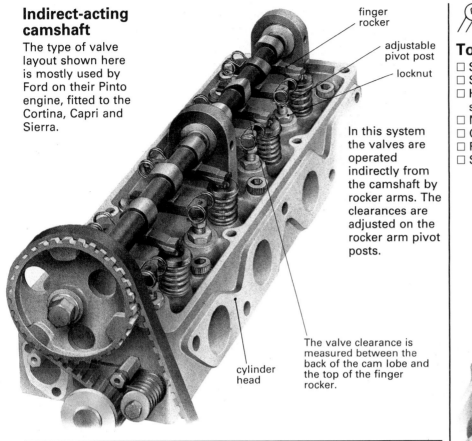

finger rocker

adjustable pivot post

locknut

cylinder head

In this system the valves are operated indirectly from the camshaft by rocker arms. The clearances are adjusted on the rocker arm pivot posts.

The valve clearance is measured between the back of the cam lobe and the top of the finger rocker.

intermediate

Tools and materials
- ☐ Spanners and sockets
- ☐ Screwdrivers
- ☐ Hammer and block of wood or soft-faced mallet
- ☐ New cam cover gasket
- ☐ Gasket jointing compound
- ☐ Feeler gauges
- ☐ Special crow's foot spanner

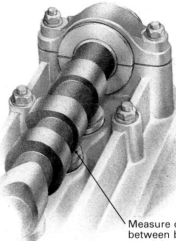

Measure clearance between back of cam lobe and tappet.

Bucket tappets

Where the camshaft acts directly on the valves via bucket tappets, the valve adjustment is made with shims. Checking the valve clearances is easy, but adjusting them means taking out the shims and, in some cases, the camshaft.

It is best to check the clearances at every service interval, and if any adjustment is needed, leave it to a garage. It generally works out cheaper and easier to have this job done by a professional.

The valve clearances on an OHC engine do not usually go out of adjustment as often as those on an OHV engine. Even so, they need to be checked at specified intervals.

In most cases you can check the clearances yourself, although you may have to leave any adjustment to a garage. The exception is a BL car fitted with an O-series engine, for which you need special tools to remove the camshaft cover.

There are two main types of overhead camshaft operation – direct-acting and indirect-acting – and the means of checking and adjusting is different for each one.

Direct acting

The direct-acting OHC engine is the more common of the two. Unfortunately the valve this engine has – the bucket tappet and shim design – is also the more difficult to adjust.

The valve clearances are set by fitting metal shims (thick washers that come in different sizes) between the camshaft and the bucket tappet, or between the bucket tappet and the valve stem.

Adjustment is a time-consuming job that involves taking out each set of old shims and fitting a set of new shims of the correct thickness. It is best left to a garage.

Some Vauxhalls use a variation on the bucket tappet and shim design where you can adjust the valve clearances yourself without taking out the shims. Instead you use an Allen key to screw a wedged adjuster under the shim to alter the clearance. This is really only for fine adjustments – if the wedge runs out of adjustment before the clearance is correct, the shims will have to be replaced by a garage.

Indirect acting

In one type of indirect-acting OHC engine, the camshaft operates the valves via finger rocker arms. The

Checking clearances: bucket and shim

Find out from your handbook whether the valve clearance is given for a hot or cold engine. If hot, run the engine until it has reached normal working temperature.

First remove the camshaft cover. Then turn the engine over (easier if you remove spark plugs first) in the normal direction of rotation using a spanner on the crankshaft pulley nut. If access to it is limited, you can turn the engine over on the fan belt or jack up one of the driving wheels and turn it with the car in fourth gear.

Turn the engine until the cam lobe of the valve you want to check is pointing directly away from the bucket tappet. Select the correct size feeler gauge and slip it into the gap between the cam lobe and the top of the tappet (see below).

If the clearance is correct, the gauge will slip easily into the gap, and there will be a slight drag on it as you try to withdraw it. On some cars there is a range of clearance allowed, so if the first size you try is too large or small, try again with another feeler that is within the clearance range.

When you have checked the first valve, turn the engine over to check all the other clearances in turn. If a clearance is outside the range allowed you should take the car to a garage for adjustment.

Removing the camshaft cover

First find all the bolts or screws that hold the cover to the engine. Using a socket, spanner or screwdriver, undo the fixings a little at a time working in sequence around the cover to avoid distorting it.

The cover should now come off. If it is stuck, don't try to lever it free with a screwdriver or you may cause damage. Instead, lightly tap it with a hammer and block of wood, or a soft-faced mallet, and lift it off.

rockers pivot on posts that can be moved up or down to adjust the clearance between the rockers and the camshaft.

The other type has rocker arms like those on an OHV engine. The adjuster is a screw and locknut arrangement in the rocker arm that bears on to the top of the valve stem. On both types you can adjust the clearances yourself.

Remove cam cover

The first job is to remove the camshaft cover from the top of the engine. It may be held by bolts or screws. On some cars you will have to take off the air filter or air filter piping to get the cam cover off. Then undo the fixings holding the cover, working in a diagonal sequence to avoid distorting it.

Lift off the cover – if it sticks, tap it very gently with a hammer and block of wood or a soft-faced mallet to jar it free. Remove the old gasket if it hasn't come off with the cover. Now you can check the clearances (see appropriate step for your car).

Refit cover

Smear a little grease or gasket jointing compound on both sides of the new gasket and lay it in place on the engine or the cover. Lower the cover on without dislodging or pinching the gasket. Refit all the bolts finger tight, then do them up to the recommended torque setting (see your manual) using a torque wrench. Work in a diagonal sequence to avoid distorting the cover.

Do the same with screws if the cover is held on by these. If the manual gives a torque setting, use the end of an impact screwdriver attached to the torque wrench.

Checking clearances: finger rockers

On an OHC engine with finger rockers, the valve clearance is measured between the back of the cam lobe and the rocker arm.

Turn the engine over (using one of the methods outlined in the sideline on the opposite page), until the cam lobe of the valve to be checked is pointing straight up.

With the engine hot or cold as required (see your handbook), slide the correct feeler gauge into the gap. If the clearance is correct, it should be a tight sliding fit (**1**).

If you need to adjust the gap, slacken off the locknut at the base of the rocker arm pivot post. Then use another spanner to screw the pivot post up or down to adjust the gap –

there are spanner flats on the pivot post.

Keep sliding the feeler in the gap while you adjust, until you can feel that it is a tight sliding fit (**2**). Hold the pivot post in position, then carefully withdraw the feeler gauge. Use another spanner to tighten the locknut (**3**), taking care not to move the pivot post. Recheck the gap afterwards.

On some Fords, such as the Cortina, Capri and Sierra you may find that the carburettor gets in the way of some of the locknuts and adjuster nuts. To get round this you can use a special 'crow's foot' spanner (see right).

☆ Special spanners

On some cars, such as Fords, you will find that you need a special crow's foot spanner to get at the adjuster nuts. These are readily available from accessory shops, dealers, and hire shops.

Although it is possible to do the job without the tool, the time and frustration it saves are probably worth the extra expense.

If you want to, you can make your own crow's foot spanner by taking an old spanner of the correct size, heating up the handle and bending it to the required shape.

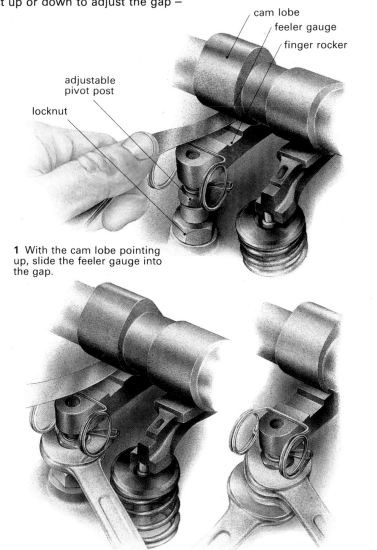

1 With the cam lobe pointing up, slide the feeler gauge into the gap.

cam lobe
feeler gauge
finger rocker

adjustable pivot post

locknut

2 Keep the feeler gauge in place while you adjust the gap.

3 Tighten the locknut with another spanner.

Checking clearances: Vauxhall engines

On some Vauxhall OHC engines you can make small adjustments to the valve clearances by means of screws that slide wedges under the shims.

Turn the engine over so that the cam lobe of the valve to be checked is pointing away from the bucket tappet. With the engine hot or cold as required (see your handbook), slide the correct feeler gauge between the back of the cam lobe and the tappet (1).

If the clearance is correct the feeler gauge should be a tight sliding fit. If the clearance needs adjusting, keep the feeler gauge in the gap, and use an Allen key to turn the adjuster (2).

When the clearance is correct, withdraw the Allen key and the feeler gauge – there is no locknut on the adjuster. If the full travel of the adjuster is not enough to set the correct clearance, have the shim replaced at a garage. Continue with the remaining valves. It may help you to keep track if you mark each cam lobe with a dab of chalk when you have adjusted it.

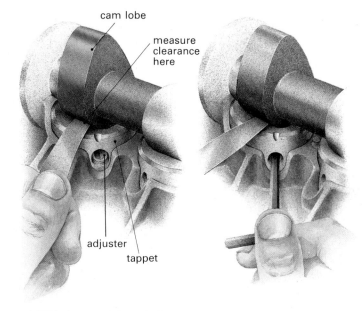

1 With the cam lobe pointing away from the tappet, slide the feeler gauge in. It should be a tight, sliding fit.

2 If you need to correct the clearance, fit an Allen key into the adjuster in the side of the tappet and turn it.

Checking clearances: rocker arm

The second type of indirect-acting OHC engine has the camshaft operating the valves via rocker arms mounted on a shaft. The adjuster is similar to that on an OHV engine: a screw and locknut located in one end of the rocker arm. Again, check in your handbook to see if the valves need to be set hot or cold.

To check the clearances, turn the engine in its normal direction of rotation until number one piston is at top dead centre (TDC) on its firing stroke. (To check which cylinder is on its firing stroke, take off the distributor cap and see which contact the rotor arm is pointing to.)

With the engine in this position, the TDC timing marks on the crankshaft pulley and engine block will align and the mark on the camshaft sprocket will be at the top. There will be a clearance between the rocker and valve stem on both valves on number one cylinder.

Check the clearance by sliding the feeler gauge in between the rocker arm and the valve stem. Check valves 1 and 2 (numbering from the front of the engine) and, without moving the engine, check valves 3 and 5. If all the gaps are correct, turn the engine one full turn so that the timing marks align again, and check valves 4, 6, 7 and 8.

If any of the valves needs adjusting, slacken the locknut on the rocker arm using a ring spanner. Use a screwdriver in the adjuster slot to alter the clearance – clockwise decreases the gap anti-clockwise increases it.

When the clearance is correct, hold the adjuster screw firm and do up the locknut. Recheck the clearance in case it slipped when you were tightening the locknut.

⚠️Turning the crankshaft

Because the crankshaft turns twice for every turn of the camshaft, it is very easy to get the valve clearances 180° out – especially if the timing marks are difficult to get at.

If you are uncertain about this, you can check the clearances using the 'rule of nine'.

With the feeler gauge still in place, adjust the clearance by turning the adjuster slot with a screwdriver.

Looking for coolant leaks

If the water level in your car's cooling system continually drops, requiring frequent topping up, then there is a leak somewhere in the system.

There are two types of cooling system – sealed and non-sealed. Sealed systems keep the coolant level topped up from a small expansion tank away from the radiator. They should never lose water. If the level goes down then there is a leak somewhere.

Non-sealed systems have no expansion tank and therefore tend to lose a little water – as the pressure in the system builds up, some water may be forced past the pressure cap and lost on to the road. Only if the need for topping up becomes more frequent than usual do you need to worry.

Leak points

A leak from the cooling system can be very difficult to find, since the coolant quickly evaporates, leaving few traces.

The most likely source of leaks is where the rubber hoses join to the engine, the radiator and the heater. Quite often the rubber deteriorates with age, allowing coolant to leak past. Alternatively, the clips may have been done up too tight, damaging the hose, or else they may have become loose.

Other danger spots are where the tanks at the top and bottom of the radiator join the radiator's finned core and where the stubs fit into the top and bottom hoses. The radiator core can also leak, although this is likely only if the core has been punctured, say, by a screwdriver.

Gaskets/core plugs

The engine itself can leak coolant both from the gaskets for the water pump and cylinder head, and from the engine core plugs.

The core plugs are dished metal

 basic

Tools and materials

- ☐ Newspaper
- ☐ Torch
- ☐ Mirror
- ☐ Screwdrivers
- ☐ Spanners
- ☐ Antifreeze hydrometer
- ☐ New antifreeze

⚠ Creeping antifreeze

Antifreeze has an uncanny ability to find any weak spot in the cooling system. Unlike water, it can 'creep' through even the smallest of holes.

This means that, if there is a leak in the cooling system, the antifreeze will start to drain away very soon after you add it.

Looking for leaks

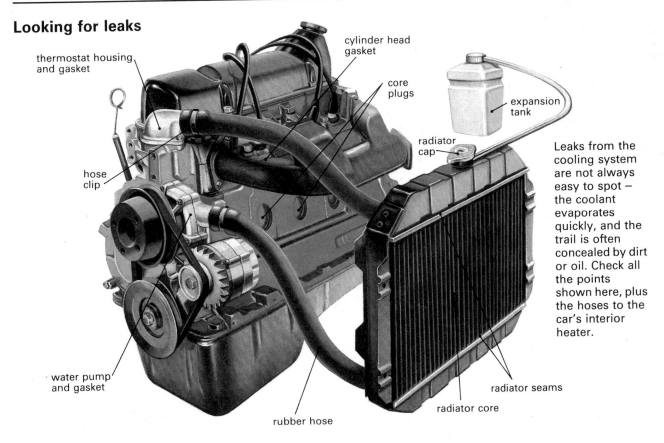

thermostat housing and gasket

cylinder head gasket

core plugs

hose clip

radiator cap

expansion tank

water pump and gasket

rubber hose

radiator core

radiator seams

Leaks from the cooling system are not always easy to spot – the coolant evaporates quickly, and the trail is often concealed by dirt or oil. Check all the points shown here, plus the hoses to the car's interior heater.

Checking the water pump

If you are losing coolant and there is a rattling or screeching noise from the front of the engine, then the water pump is failing.

To check it, loosen the drive belt, then try to rock the fan back and forwards (below). Any movement means that the bearings are worn.

If the fan is not fitted to the water pump, then loosen the drive belt and try to rock the pulley (below). Again, any movement means worn bearings.

The water pump shaft rocking on its bearings will eventually rupture the water seal inside – if it hasn't already done so. To check this, look underneath the pump. If the seal has gone, you will see a rusty trail where water has been leaking out of the small hole in the pump body.

Always fit a new water pump, as the wear or leakage will only become worse. Eventually the pump will fail completely, and may leave you stranded.

discs which fill holes in the engine block left over from the casting process. Sometimes they simply come loose under pressure, but they are just as likely to have corroded through, especially if there is not enough antifreeze in the coolant. Core plugs are often well hidden on the engine and difficult to find.

Internal leakage

Finally there are internal leaks – leaks inside the engine. These can be between the cooling system and the lubrication system, or between the cooling system and the cylinders. The most common cause is failure of the cylinder head gasket, but sometimes a cracked cylinder block may be responsible.

Finding the leak

The first step is to find the general area where the leak is coming from. This makes it easier to trace the source of the leak. Always work with the engine hot and the pressure in the cooling system built-up. This will force any coolant out at the weak spot.

Switch off the engine and look all over the engine, radiator, rubber hoses and water pump for tell-tale signs of a leak, such as rusty water trails or bluish-white antifreeze trails. If none is evident, lay a few sheets of newspaper underneath the engine, start it up again and leave it to run – any drips will land on the paper, and you should then be able to pinpoint the trouble area.

Once you know the general area use a torch to scan carefully all the likely troublespots – take care not

Check the hoses

Leaks from hoses can often be cured simply by tightening up the clips a little. If the hose still leaks, it is best to fit a new one together with new hose clips.

to burn yourself. A mirror is very useful for examining inaccessible corners, especially when you check the core plugs.

On some BL cars fitted with the A-series engine, such as earlier Minis, there is a small rubber hose hidden beneath the cylinder head. This is very prone to damage, so make sure you check it. Later Minis and other BL cars fitted with the A+ series engine do not have this hose.

If the leak is not too serious and is in an expensive component such as the radiator, you may be able to cure the problem by using a proprietary leak sealer.

Testing antifreeze strength

To test the antifreeze strength you must use a special antifreeze hydrometer, not a battery one.

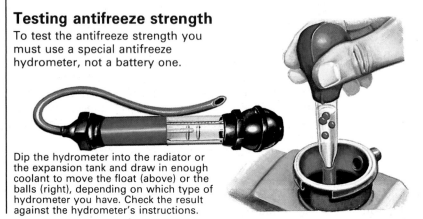

Dip the hydrometer into the radiator or the expansion tank and draw in enough coolant to move the float (above) or the balls (right), depending on which type of hydrometer you have. Check the result against the hydrometer's instructions.

Fitting a new water pump

Water pump location

water pump

cooling fan

drive belt

bottom hose

On most cars the pump is at the front of the engine, driven by the generator drive belt.

The water pump drives coolant around the cooling system to stop the engine overheating. It is a very simple unit, usually driven from the generator drive belt. The pump can, with time, develop a leak – if your car continually loses water, yet there are no obvious leaks, then you should check the water pump.

The other problem that affects the water pump is worn bearings as a result of the generator drive belt being overtightened. If the bearings are worn they will screech or rattle (see sideline, right).

Check for leaks

Warm the engine up so that the cooling system is pressurized, then stop the engine. Have a look for water running out of the pump body via a small hole located just below the pump spindle. If there is any trace of water, the gland seal has failed and you need to fit a new water pump.

Before you remove the pump you should drain the cooling system. On

some cars it is possible to remove the pump with the radiator still in place. However, the job is a lot easier if you take the radiator out first. It also means there is less danger of accidentally puncturing the radiator if a spanner or screwdriver slips.

Remove fan

First slacken the generator fixings and remove the drive belt. If your car has a mechanical or viscous-coupled fan, you need to remove the fan blades. The new pump won't come with these fitted, although the viscous-coupled type may come with a new coupling built into the pump.

The blades are usually held on by bolts running through into a flange on the pump spindle. They also hold on the pump pulley. On cars with an electric fan, only the pulley is held by these bolts.

On some cars the water pump casing forms the mounting for the generator pivot bolts.

If yours is like this, you may

Tools and materials

□ New water pump plus gasket and jointing compound
□ Screwdrivers
□ Spanners and sockets
□ Container for coolant
□ Soft-faced hammer
□ Clean rags
□ Blunt scraper tool
□ New hoses and fresh antifreeze as required

Cam belt drive

On some cars the water pump is turned not by the generator drive belt, but by the camshaft drive belt. Once you have removed the cam belt cover (above) you can get to the pump (see pages 35, 36).

Failed bearings

To check whether the water pump bearings have failed, slacken and remove the drive belt then start the engine and run it for a few seconds. If the noise now stops it is probably coming from the water pump bearings, though it could be coming from the generator.

To double check, try to rock the fan blades from side to side. If you can feel play, the pump bearings are worn. If not, spin the fan or pulley by hand. If it rotates smoothly and silently, the generator bearings are at fault.

need to remove the generator from the car.

Disconnect hoses

The pump is connected to the cooling system by the hoses – first disconnect the bottom hose if you haven't already done so. Next look to see which other hoses are connected to the pump – for example, the heater hoses – and undo them. On BL cars with an A-series engine, there is a small transfer (bypass) hose running between the water pump and engine block.

Now undo all the bolts holding the pump to the engine a little at a time, working in sequence around the pump. Once all the bolts are loosened, spin them out.

The pump will probably be stuck in place, so give it a sharp blow with a soft-faced hammer. Lift the pump off. Block off the hole in the engine block with a rag, and use a blunt scraper tool to remove all traces of the old gasket.

Fit new pump

Smear a little gasket jointing compound on to both sides of the new water pump gasket. Place the gasket on the pump or engine (whichever is the easier) ensuring that all the bolt holes line up. Refit the pump to the engine and loosely replace all the bolts. On an A-series engine, it is well worth fitting a new transfer hose because it is quite prone to leaking. Make sure the hose fits tightly over the stubs on the pump and the engine block.

Do up all the bolts tightly to hold the pump. Refit all the hoses – if any look at all suspect fit new ones. Refit the water pump pulley and the fan and do up the bolts, then refit the generator if you removed it.

Refit and tension the drive belt then refit the radiator.

Refill the cooling system with a water/antifreeze mix, then start the engine and run it to check for leaks.

Step-by-step water pump removal

Undo the bolts holding the fan to the water pump flange – remove all the bolts, noting the position of any washers or spacers.

Lift the fan away from the water pump, again noting whether there are any spacers between the fan and the water pump flange.

Pull off the water pump pulley from the pump flange – if you haven't already taken off the drive belt, it can come off with the pulley.

Disconnect any other hoses that are attached to the water pump; here a heater hose is being disconnected from its stub.

Slacken off all the bolts securing the pump to the engine block. Once they are all loose, remove them by hand.

Lift the pump away from the engine – if it is stuck, jar it free. Remove all traces of old gasket from the engine block.

Fitting new core plugs to the engine

Plug locations

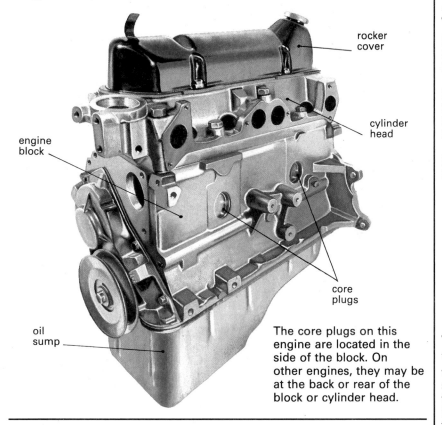

- rocker cover
- cylinder head
- engine block
- core plugs
- oil sump

The core plugs on this engine are located in the side of the block. On other engines, they may be at the back or rear of the block or cylinder head.

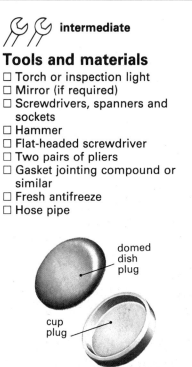
- domed dish plug
- cup plug

Types of core plug

Your engine will probably be fitted with one of the types of core plug shown above. The domed dish plug fits into a shallow seating and is hit hard so that it expands to fit tightly in the engine block. The cup plug is a tight push-fit into its hole in the engine block.

Core plugs are metal discs that are set into the engine block at various points. They seal holes provided in the block and head to allow these to be cast, and they also act as weak points in the cooling system that can give way if the coolant overheats or freezes.

However, because they are weak points, the plugs may leak or blow out at the wrong time. The most common fault is a plug that corrodes from the inside out, finally developing a small leak. In a few cases the plug may actually loosen and fall out, dumping the coolant on to the road – an expensive business if you don't stop rapidly.

When to check

It is worth checking the core plugs about twice a year to see if they are leaking. They are usually in the sides and front or rear of the cylinder block, and in the front or rear of the cylinder head. They may be awkwardly placed close to the walls of the engine compartment, so if you cannot find them, ask your dealer where they are.

Examine the plugs

First look for signs of rusty water trails or antifreeze trails running down from the plug. If you see either, the plug has a leak.

If there are no trails, carefully examine each plug using a torch or an inspection light and a mirror if necessary. Look for signs of rust bubbling on the core plug.

Also check whether the plug seems to be firmly held in the block – a ring of rusty water around the edge means it is working loose and may blow out fairly soon.

Approaches

How you replace the leaking or damaged plug depends on its location. If you can get at it with a

☆ Finding hidden plugs

You may find that the location of the core plugs makes them difficult to see. If so, use a mirror and torch to help you inspect them.

Awkward plugs

You may find that, although you can get the old plug out, there isn't enough room to hammer in the new plug. The only way you can do this is to take the engine out of the car.

BL cars with an in-line B-series engine, for example, have a dish-type plug fitted just in front of the bulkhead and masked by the engine backplate. But in this case you make use of a hole located in the backplate (facing the starter) to help when refitting the plug.

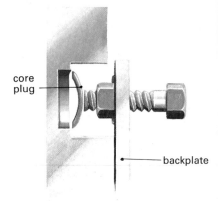

core plug

backplate

Insert the new plug into its hole in the block, then pass a 2in (50mm) bolt through the hole in the backplate. Fit a nut and washer on the other side, tighten it up, then screw the bolt up so that it presses the plug firmly into its seat.

Carry on until the plug has a slight dent in the centre – it is then sealed into the block. Now unscrew the bolt, remove the nut and washer and take out the bolt.

You may be able to adapt this method for replacing other awkward core plugs.

hammer, you can replace it yourself without difficulty. If access is restricted only by a readily unbolted component, again you can do the job yourself.

If the plug faces the engine compartment wall, it is usually unreachable. If it's in the cylinder head, the cylinder head must be removed. If it's in the engine block, the whole engine will have to come out of the car – you may want to leave this job to a garage.

Drain coolant

Start by disconnecting the battery earth lead, then draining the cooling system.

Whichever type of core plug your engine has (see sideline, previous page), the job of removing it is much the same. The easiest way is to hammer a screwdriver through the plug and lever it out.

If it is a cup plug and the edges stick out from the surface of the engine block, you may be able to pull it out with two pairs of pliers. Grip the edges of the plug firmly and pull with an even amount of force on both pliers. Do not lever against the engine block – you may damage the plug's seating.

Fit new plug

Use a slim screwdriver to clean the plug's seat in the engine block. Smear the edges of the new plug with gasket jointing compound or a similar gasket sealant.

Push the plug into its hole in the engine block. If it is a dish-type plug, make sure the domed side is outwards. Use a hammer and a large diameter flat-headed punch to hit the plug exactly in its middle. This will expand the plug into the hole, making it a tight fit. For a cup-type plug, put a snug-fitting socket into the cup, then hammer the socket to drive the plug fully home. If access is impossible, see sideline, left.

Refill the cooling system – first flush the system using a hose pipe, then refill with a fresh water/antifreeze mixture. Start the engine and let it warm up to its normal operating temperature. Check there are no leaks from the plug.

Removing and replacing the plugs

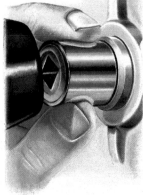

You may be able to pull out a cup-type plug with pliers.

Knock a screwdriver through the plug, and lever the plug out of the engine.

To fit a cup plug, drift it home with a hammer and socket.

To fit a dish plug, hit it in the middle with a punch to expand it into the hole.

Checking cylinder compression

If your engine persistently misfires, or lacks power, yet the ignition system and fuel supply are in good order, then the fault probably lies inside the cylinders.

To find out which cylinder is causing the problem, you need to carry out a compression test. This measures the amount of pressure produced by each piston going up and down in its cylinder. For this you will need a compression tester, which you can hire or buy quite cheaply.

Prepare the engine

Run the engine until it reaches its normal operating temperature (until the needle on the temperature gauge reaches the normal sector). Do not do the tests with the engine cold, or the readings will be false. Once the engine has warmed up, switch off then remove all the spark plug leads.

Next clean all around the spark plugs with an old paint brush to remove loose dirt. Now remove the plug from cylinder number 1 (usually the one nearest the crankshaft pulley) using a proper spark plug spanner.

Testing each cylinder

Screw in the tester or hold it over the plug hole, depending on the type of tester. If you have the push-fit type, you will need a helper to do the test. Now you or your helper should press the accelerator pedal right down to the floor and hold it there. This ensures that plenty of air

basic

Tools and materials

☐ Paint brush
☐ Spark plug
☐ Compression tester
☐ Clean engine oil
☐ Notepad and pen

⚠ Precautions

Before doing this test you should disconnect one of the low tension (LT) leads from the coil. This will prevent any sparks accidentally jumping from the spark plug caps into the engine and possibly causing an explosion.

If your car has fuel injection, look in your car handbook to see which fuse covers the petrol pump and remove that fuse from the fusebox.

Taking the readings

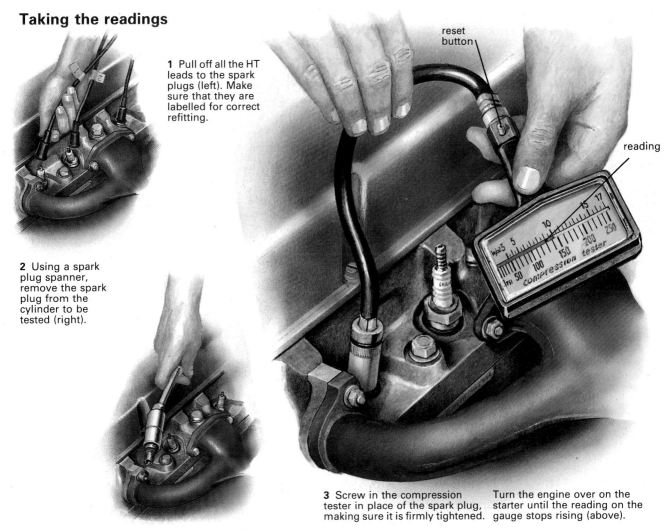

1 Pull off all the HT leads to the spark plugs (left). Make sure that they are labelled for correct refitting.

2 Using a spark plug spanner, remove the spark plug from the cylinder to be tested (right).

reset button

reading

3 Screw in the compression tester in place of the spark plug, making sure it is firmly tightened.

Turn the engine over on the starter until the reading on the gauge stops rising (above).

screw-in tester

push-fit tester

Compression testers

There are two types of tester – screw-in and push-fit. The screw-in type is the easiest to use and has a threaded end which fits in place of the spark plug. This leaves you free to operate the starter yourself.

The push-fit type has a rubber plug on the end which has to be held in the spark plug hole by hand. You will need a helper to turn the engine over for you.

With both types, a reset button is fitted to zero the gauge ready for the next test.

☆ Using a vacuum gauge

It is possible to check the engine condition by using a vacuum gauge, if one is fitted to your car.

If the needle of the gauge drops to zero when the engine is idling, and returns to 22 when the engine is running fast (above left), the piston rings are probably worn.

When the needle drifts between 5 and 19 (above right), the cause may be a compression leak in the cylinder head gasket between two or more cylinders.

gets into the cylinders for an accurate reading.

Turn the ignition key to operate the starter motor. Let the engine turn for five to ten revolutions, or about six to eight seconds, or until the reading in the gauge stops rising. Keep well clear of all moving parts.

Make a note of the maximum pressure and how long it took to get that reading. Then press the reset button to zero the gauge, replace the spark plug, and test the other cylinders in order. Ensure you allow the same number of revolutions or time for each cylinder or the readings will be inaccurate.

Analyse the results

The figures you get should all be within 10 per cent of each other, and within 10 per cent of the manufacturer's figures. See your handbook or ask your dealer.

Identical, but low readings on all cylinders point to a well-worn engine. A low reading on two adjacent cylinders (say numbers 2 and 3) indicates a failed cylinder head gasket, or a cracked cylinder head or cylinder block between those two cylinders.

If just one cylinder has a low reading, then the problem lies in that cylinder. You can confirm exactly what the problem is by doing what is called a wet compression test (usually just called a wet test).

Wet test

Pour about a dessert spoonful of clean engine oil (or give a couple of squirts with your oil can) into the cylinder to be checked. Refit the compression tester and do the tests as before.

If there is a marked increase in the reading, then it is highly likely that the piston rings are worn (the oil acts as a seal around the rings, temporarily increasing the pressure). If the reading does not increase, then the piston may have a hole in it, the cylinder bore may be very badly damaged or – more likely – the cylinder head gasket or the valves may be faulty.

If the head gasket has 'blown' you may already have noticed other problems with your car, such as overheating, misfiring or water loss. If so, check the gasket.

If a valve is faulty it tends to cause misfiring and sometimes a 'chuffing' sound through the exhaust. Check the valves if necessary.

Screw-in testers

Most spark plugs have a 14mm thread, but your car may be fitted with 18mm, 12mm or 10mm plugs. If you hire a screw-in tester, make sure it has the right size thread for your plug, or that it can be fitted with an adapter of the right size. You may also need to fit a long-reach adapter if your spark plugs are deeply recessed.

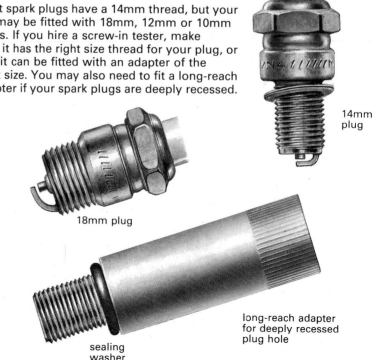

14mm plug

18mm plug

long-reach adapter for deeply recessed plug hole

sealing washer

Replacing manifold gaskets

Manifold arrangements

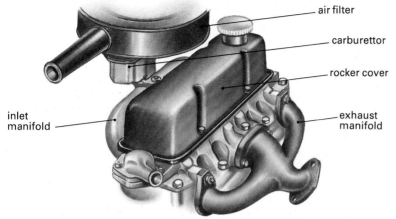

air filter

carburettor

rocker cover

exhaust manifold

inlet manifold

The inlet and exhaust manifolds may be mounted on opposite sides of the engine, as here, in which case the engine is said to be crossflow. Or they may be on the same side of the engine, called non-crossflow.

The inlet and exhaust manifolds are sealed with gaskets where they join the engine's inlet and exhaust ports. The gaskets prevent loss of gases – fuel/air mixture on one side and exhaust gases on the other.

These gaskets eventually fail; the exhaust manifold gasket usually going first because of the heat of the exhaust gases. A failed exhaust manifold gasket reveals itself by a 'chuffing' sound coming from the exhaust manifold.

Symptoms of a failed inlet manifold gasket are the engine running badly and tending to stall because the gasket is letting air into the system and weakening the fuel/air mixture.

General points

On crossflow engines the inlet and exhaust manifolds are on opposite sides of the engine, while on non-crossflow engines they are on the same side. If the manifolds are on the same side, they may be joined together or separate.

Give the securing bolts or nuts a soaking in penetrating oil a few hours before you start to take off the manifolds – make sure the engine is cool before you spray.

Replacing the gasket is much the same whether on an inlet or an exhaust manifold. The main differences are in how you take off each manifold in the first place.

advanced

Tools and materials
- [ ] Penetrating oil
- [ ] Sockets and spanners
- [ ] Pencil or bung
- [ ] New downpipe gasket, if needed
- [ ] Straight edge, such as a steel rule
- [ ] New manifold gasket or gaskets
- [ ] Torque wrench
- [ ] New manifolds, if necessary

☆ Listen to the leak

You can often track down the leak with a piece of rubber tubing. Hold one end of the tube to the gasket (with the manifold still on the engine and the engine running), while you listen down the other end. Follow the gasket round the manifold until you hear a hissing noise that indicates a leak.

Confirm this by placing a small amount of oil where the leak seems to be coming from – either brush it on or apply it with a small oil can. If there is a leak, the oil will be sucked into the manifold when you run the engine.

Do not try to use this technique on the exhaust manifold – if you do you will get a painful burst of hot exhaust gases in your ear.

Removing an exhaust manifold

Apply penetrating oil to free the manifold nuts or bolts (**1**). Release the downpipe from the manifold then undo the manifold nuts or bolts with a socket spanner (**2**).

Lift the manifold and check that its face is flat (**3**). If it is, and the manifold is in good condition, scrape off the old gasket and fit the new one.

1 Spray the manifold nuts or bolts with penetrating oil (below).

2 Undo the manifold nuts or bolts with a socket spanner (above).

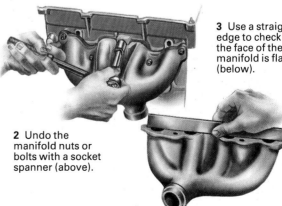

3 Use a straight edge to check that the face of the manifold is flat (below).

Removing an inlet manifold

Remove the air filter and disconnect the carburettor linkages.

Undo any hoses joined to the manifold – such as the water-heating hoses (**1**) and the brake servo hose.

Then use a socket or spanner to undo the manifold's securing nuts or bolts (**2**). Lift the manifold off the engine (**3**) and remove the old gasket (**4**).

Scrape both faces to remove all traces of the old gasket, taking care not to drop any bits down into the engine itself.

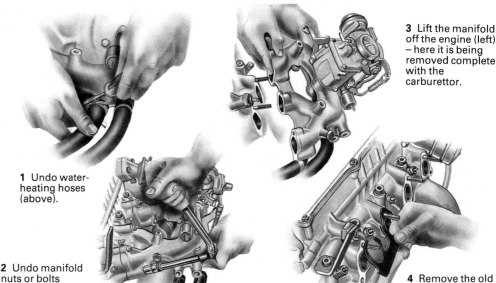

3 Lift the manifold off the engine (left) – here it is being removed complete with the carburettor.

1 Undo water-heating hoses (above).

2 Undo manifold nuts or bolts (right).

4 Remove the old gasket (left).

inlet port

V-engine manifolds

Engines with the V configuration have an exhaust manifold on each side of the engine, but there is usually just one inlet manifold situated in the centre of the 'V'.

On some V engines, the inlet manifold has one large gasket covering all the ports; on others there are two gaskets, one for each side of the engine.

Inlet manifold

Remove the air filter. Make a careful note of all connections to the carburettor then disconnect the throttle and choke cables or the pipes on an automatic choke.

Take off the fuel pipe – if possible, keep the disconnected end of the fuel pipe higher than the level of the fuel tank, or block the end of the pipe with a pencil or some other sort of bung.

You may need to remove the carburettor completely to give yourself enough room to take out the inlet manifold. If so, take care not to damage the carburettor mounting block, which may be made of rubber or some composition material and acts as a gasket.

Disconnect all hoses from the manifold. There may be a brake servo hose to disconnect and also a water hose if the manifold is water-cooled (if it is, drain the cooling system first). Now undo the nuts or bolts holding the manifold, and remove it from the engine bay.

Exhaust manifold

Check that there is enough movement at the front of the exhaust downpipe (where the manifold connects) to allow you to manoeuvre the manifold away. If there isn't, undo the bracket holding the down-pipe to the engine or gearbox.

Then undo the bolts holding the manifold to the engine and swing it away from the block. If there isn't room to do this, you will have to detach the downpipe and remove the manifold completely from the engine bay.

Checks

First check the manifold – inlet or exhaust – for cracks or other damage. Use a straight edge to make sure it is not warped. If it is damaged, you need to replace it.

Scrape off all traces of the old gasket from both the manifold and the engine ports. Block the ports with rags to stop bits of gasket falling into the engine.

Then fit the new gasket – it may come in parts. If it is a water-heated inlet manifold, you may need to apply gasket sealant to each side of the gasket – look in your manual or check with your local dealer.

Reassemble the manifold to the engine, and tighten the nuts or bolts to the correct torque setting with a torque wrench. You may need to tighten in a specific order, usually from the centre of the manifold outwards. Check in your manual or with a dealer.

Reattach all the pipes and cables and warm up the engine before rechecking the torque settings.

OHV cylinder head – removal and refitting

Typical cylinder head

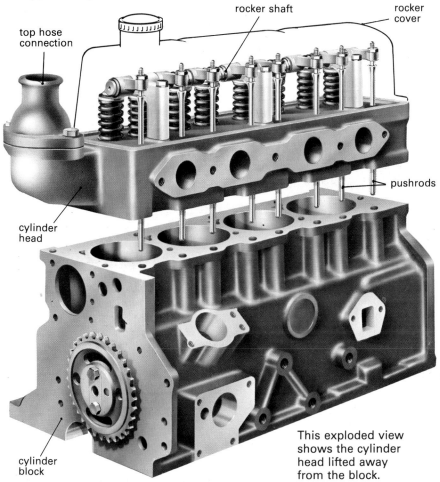

rocker shaft

rocker cover

top hose connection

cylinder head

pushrods

cylinder block

This exploded view shows the cylinder head lifted away from the block.

 **advanced**

Tools and materials

- ☐ Spanners, sockets and screwdrivers
- ☐ Bucket for draining coolant
- ☐ Decoke gasket set (contains all gaskets required)
- ☐ Soft-faced mallet or hammer and block of wood
- ☐ Long dowels
- ☐ Wood to support cylinder head
- ☐ Torque wrench
- ☐ Feeler gauges for resetting valves

Removing the rocker cover

Before you can take the rocker cover off, you may first have to remove items such as the air filter casing, choke and throttle linkages, vacuum advance piping, and even the distributor. You also need to disconnect any breather pipes running from the rocker cover to the carburettor or inlet manifold. Make a note of where each part goes to avoid confusion when refitting.

Then undo the fixings holding the rocker cover. There may be two bolts or nuts at the centre top of the cover (see above), or a series of fixings around the rim. Rim fixings may be screws, nuts or bolts, or special twelve-sided 'Torx' bolts.

Lift the cover off, together with its gasket.

Removing a cylinder head is a difficult job. On early cars it used to be necessary to do this regularly to decarbonize (decoke) the engine. Modern engines, however, can run to very high mileages without requiring a decoke. This means you do not have to take off the cylinder head more often than about every 50,000 miles (80,000km), unless you have a blown cylinder head gasket or a faulty inlet or exhaust valve.

Before you remove a cylinder head you should disconnect and remove the battery. Then drain the cooling system, undo the hose-clips and disconnect the top hose from the thermostat housing and radiator.

On a BL A-series engine, use a slim screwdriver to disconnect the bypass hose connecting the cylinder head to the water pump.

Next undo the nuts, bolts or clamps holding the exhaust manifold to the downpipe. If the manifold is a tubular design that fits straight on to the cylinder head, undo the nuts or bolts holding it and carefully prise the manifold away. You may need to tie or wedge it back.

Rocker cover

Now take off the rocker cover. If it is masked by the air filter, remove that first. With the air filter out of the way, make a note of any linkages that cross over, or are attached to, the rocker cover. Carefully disconnect each one, along with the fuel inlet pipe at the carburettor – plug the open end with a pencil.

Now undo all the bolts or screws

Shaftless rockers

On Vauxhall engines fitted with shaftless rockers, there is no need to take the rockers right off to remove the pushrods or cylinder head. All you need do is slacken off the central nut on each rocker until you can rotate it enough to remove the pushrod.

holding the rocker cover to the engine and lift the cover off.

On some cars the distributor gets in the way of the rocker cover so you have to remove it. Disconnect the HT leads from the coil and spark plugs and the LT lead(s) at the distributor body. Undo the clamp or bolts holding the distributor and lift it right out.

Now look at how the rocker shaft is held on to the cylinder head. With most designs the rocker shaft has its own bolts and can be removed alone. But on Leyland A- and B-series engines the cylinder head nuts also hold the rocker shaft on and you can't remove the rocker shaft until you've undone the nuts (see opposite page).

Rocker shaft

To remove the rocker shaft, undo each nut or bolt by a quarter of a turn, starting in the centre and working out until the pressure is released and you can remove the bolts by hand. Lift up the shaft slowly.

If any of the pushrods try to come up with the shaft, stop lifting and let them drop back into their holes. For Vauxhalls, see sideline, left.

Pushrods

Now take out the pushrods. Lift each pushrod up a fraction, twiddling it from side to side to break the oil seal that holds it to its cam follower deep inside the engine. If you pull the rod straight out, it might pull the cam follower up and out of its hole. On some engines it is impossible to refit the follower without dismantling the whole engine.

Keep the pushrods in order so you can put each one back in the same place (see sideline on the opposite page).

Cylinder head

The cylinder head is now held to the engine only by its bolts or nuts. The nuts have to be undone in a specific sequence to avoid distorting the metal of the cylinder head. This sequence is very important – it is usually given in your service manual or, failing that, you can ask your dealer for it.

Using a socket and T-bar or ratchet, undo each bolt by half of one turn, following the sequence strictly. If the fixings are very tight,

Removing the rocker shaft

1 Undo the nuts or bolts holding the rocker shaft to the cylinder head. Undo each fixing by a quarter of a turn each time, starting in the middle and working out to the ends.

2 Once the shaft is no longer under pressure, screw all the bolts out by hand. Slowly lift the shaft straight up and off, making sure no pushrods are coming up with it.

extend the handle with a length of tube for leverage.

Carry on undoing the fixings until you can remove each one by hand. Make a note of where each one goes because they may be of different sizes, especially if they are bolts. One way to avoid losing them and, at the same time, to remember in which order to replace them, is to stick them through a sheet of card with the cylinder head drawn on it.

On BL A- and B-series engines you can now lift off the rocker shaft and remove the pushrods (as already described).

The cylinder head is likely to be stuck fast on the cylinder block (especially if the fixings are studs with nuts on them). To remove it, first try pulling it firmly, straight up – it helps if you get a friend to pull at one end while you pull at the other. If that doesn't work, get your friend to pull up while you jar the head at various points with a soft-faced mallet or a hammer and block of wood. Don't use a metal hammer

directly on the cylinder head or you may crack the casting, and don't lever the head up with a screwdriver or you will damage the mating area of cylinder head and engine block.

Last resort

If by now the cylinder head still has not come off, you will have to resort to one final, brutal method. Refit and reconnect the battery. Carefully turn the engine over on the starter for a couple of turns. The compression pressure caused by the pistons moving up will free off the cylinder head.

Lift the head up and carefully place it on several blocks of wood to avoid damage. Remove the cylinder head gasket from the engine block.

Refitting the head

Ensure that the faces of the cylinder head and engine block are scrupu-

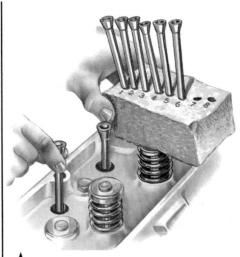

☆ Pushrod keeper

When you remove the pushrods, it is very important to remember the order in which they came out. Each must go back in the exact place it came from.

It is a good idea to push each one, as you take it out, through a piece of foam or card marked with the pushrod numbers.

Removing the head

1 Disconnect any linkages that are attached to the carburettor or cylinder head. Don't forget coolant hoses. Also release the exhaust pipe connection.

2 You need to follow a strict sequence for undoing the bolts, normally working from the middle outwards – look in your service manual or check with your dealer.

lously clean. A small speck of dirt can be enough to make the gasket leak, and it will need renewing within a short space of time.

Lay the gasket, face upwards, on the engine block. Some are marked 'top' or 'up' on the upper face.

Lower the cylinder head on to the gasket being careful not to dislodge it. If this is very difficult (as it will be on cars with cylinder head bolts), put a long dowel into each of the end bolt holes, then fit the cylinder head over them.

Refit the cylinder head nuts or bolts and their washers – remember to take out the dowels if you used them. Make sure that each fixing is in the position it came from. On BL A- and B-series engines, refit the pushrods and rocker shaft before fitting the head nuts and bolts.

Refer to the head tightening sequence for your car, and do the bolts up to the correct tightness with a torque wrench. If only one figure is given, do each bolt up to half the figure, then work round in sequence again to the correct torque.

Some cars have a torque figure followed by a figure in degrees: 30lb ft + 90° for example. This means you tighten the bolts to that torque, then turn each bolt, in sequence, a further 90° (one quarter of a turn).

Finishing off

Once the bolts are done up, refit the pushrods and rocker shaft, and set the valve clearances (see pages 5, 6, 7, 8). Fit a new rocker cover gasket, and fit the cover.

If you had to remove the distributor, you'll need to refit it and reset the timing from scratch. Also connect the vacuum advance pipe to the distributor.

Refit the exhaust pipe with a new gasket if it uses one. Make sure all the joints are gas-tight. Check the air filter then refit it (or a new one) and its casing.

Reconnect the fuel pipe to the carburettor, and the throttle and choke linkages. Start the engine and check that it runs quietly and smoothly. You may need to retune the carburettor.

Most cars need the cylinder head bolts checked and retightened after about 500 miles (800km). Don't avoid doing this, it's very important. If you fail to retighten the bolts the head gasket may soon blow.

Refitting the cylinder head

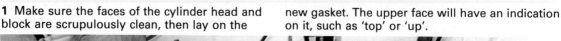

1 Make sure the faces of the cylinder head and block are scrupulously clean, then lay on the new gasket. The upper face will have an indication on it, such as 'top' or 'up'.

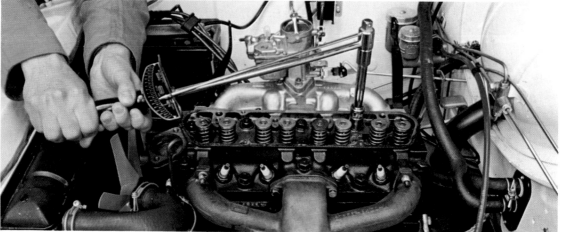

2 Lay down the head and refit the cylinder head bolts, following the correct tightening sequence. Use a torque wrench to get tightness correct – see your handbook for the figure.

Cylinder head removal on an OHC engine

If your car is overheating because of a blown head gasket, or if a compression test shows that there is a loss of compression through the valves, then you have to remove the cylinder head to fix the problem.

Taking off the cylinder head from an overhead cam engine is a little more difficult than on an overhead valve engine because you need to disconnect the timing chain or belt between the crankshaft and camshaft. This has to be carefully reset when refitting.

Preliminaries

Let the engine cool down. Start by draining the cooling system. Remove the top hose running between the radiator and the cylinder head, then disconnect the heater hoses if they connect to the cylinder head or if they look as if they may get in your way.

If working space is restricted it is best to remove the radiator altogether to prevent it being damaged.

Next disconnect the exhaust manifold from the exhaust system front pipe. This may be a simple clamp connection, or there may be nuts holding two flanges.

Now remove the air filter and have a look at the carburettor to see how it fits. If you are lucky there may be enough space to disconnect

advanced

Tools and materials

☐ Spanners and screwdrivers
☐ Sockets
☐ Special Allen or Torx drive keys, if required
☐ Container for coolant
☐ String
☐ Decoke gasket set
☐ Gasket jointing compound
☐ Torque wrench

Chain-driven overhead camshaft

Where the camshaft is chain driven, the chain runs round a sprocket bolted to the front of the camshaft.

Releasing a timing chain is a little more complicated than freeing a belt because you have to be careful not to let the chain slip into the sump.

Belt-driven overhead cam cylinder head

To remove the cylinder head, you first need to disconnect all the components shown here.

The most important part of the job is to align the engine timing marks before you remove the timing belt.

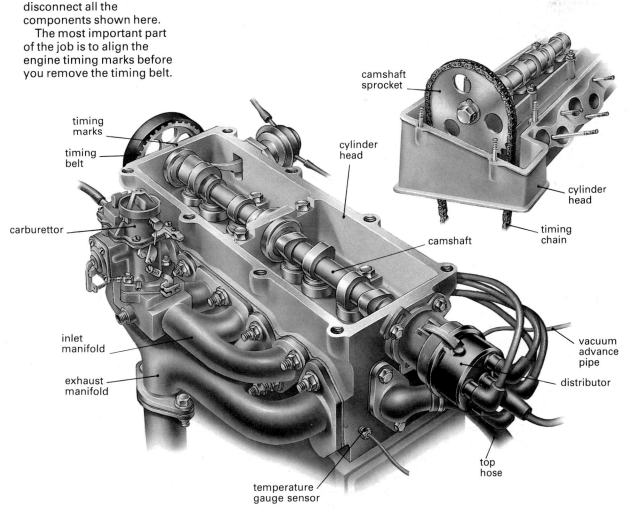

timing marks

timing belt

carburettor

inlet manifold

exhaust manifold

temperature gauge sensor

cylinder head

camshaft

top hose

vacuum advance pipe

distributor

camshaft sprocket

cylinder head

timing chain

Size up the job

In the vast majority of cars, you will have no problems getting the cylinder head off. But on a few cars, such as the Hillman Imp and Talbot Samba, the working space is so cramped that you may find it easier to remove the engine first. If you are in any doubt as to what you should do, consult your dealer or a workshop manual.

Another point to watch for is that more and more manufacturers are using specially shaped bolts to secure the cylinder head. These bolts resemble Allen bolts but have a star-shaped drive. They are called Torx bolts and you need a special Torx drive key (from an accessory shop or dealer) to remove them.

Removing a camshaft carrier

On some engines the camshaft masks some of the cylinder head bolts, and you cannot remove the bolts without first removing the camshaft.

If yours is like this, you need to unbolt the camshaft bearings (above) or the camshaft carrier (below) and lift it off. If the bucket tappets are left loose, lift off each one in turn and place it in a numbered jar to ensure correct refitting.

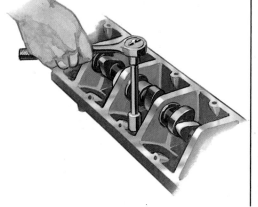

Disconnect ancillaries

Drain the cooling system, then disconnect the top hose (**1**) and any heater hoses. Release the exhaust manifold to downpipe connection (**2**), and disconnect and take off the carburettor (**3**). Unbolt the manifolds and remove them.

1 Remove the top hose.

2 Unscrew the clamp holding the exhaust manifold to the downpipe.

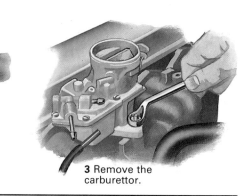

3 Remove the carburettor.

the manifold from the cylinder head and swing it to one side of the engine bay. This avoids having to disconnect the throttle and choke cables and the fuel pipes.

If this is not possible, disconnect the fuel pipe (or pipes) from the carburettor and plug the open ends with pencil stubs. Release the throttle linkage (and choke cable where fitted). If your car has an automatic choke, disconnect the wire or the coolant pipes.

Undo the bolts holding the carburettor and remove it. If you want to, you can now undo the bolts holding the inlet and exhaust manifolds to the cylinder head and remove them. Alternatively, you can leave the manifolds attached as they may provide a useful lever with which to lift the head off.

Disconnect electrics

Number the spark plug leads to ensure you refit them in the correct order, then disconnect them. Where the leads pass through guides on the cylinder head, release them. If the distributor is mounted on the cylinder head, release the low-tension wire or wires from it. These may be single connections or a multi-connector plug.

Also remove the vacuum advance pipe. Find where the temperature gauge wire fits to the sensor unit in the cylinder head, and gently pull it off. You should now have cleared the area around the cylinder head and be ready to work on the head itself.

Set the timing

Before you can remove the timing belt or chain you must set the engine correctly to avoid the risk of damaging it afterwards.

This is done by aligning timing marks on the camshaft and crankshaft pulleys when the engine is at top dead centre.

Refer to your handbook or service manual to see where the timing marks are on your car. On a belt-driven cam, you now have to remove the timing belt cover; on a chain-driven cam, the cam cover has to come off.

The cam cover is normally secured by a number of screws, bolts or Torx bolts. Undo them and lift the cover off. Now align the timing marks by turning the engine over with a spanner on the crankshaft pulley, or alternatively put the car in gear, release the handbrake and push or pull the car until the marks align.

Check in which direction the rotor arm is pointing. On most cars the rotor arm should point towards the high-tension lead to number one cylinder but check with your manual as a few cars use a different cylinder for the timing.

On the BL O-series engine, the camshaft timing mark is correctly aligned at 90 degrees BTDC, so the rotor arm will be pointing at number two cylinder position.

If the rotor arm is not pointing in the right direction, turn the engine over by one of the methods described above until the arm points towards the mark you made earlier. Put the handbrake on and the car in gear to stop it accidentally turning.

Pull off belt/chain

Most belts are held taut by a tensioning device so slacken it off (see pages 35, 36, 37, 38). Then pull the belt off the camshaft pulley and allow it to dangle from the crankshaft pulley at the bottom of the engine.

On engines with a chain you usually have to remove the camshaft sprocket from the camshaft. Before you remove the sprocket, pack a cloth around the sprocket and chain assembly to prevent anything from dropping down into the engine.

Ask a friend to grasp the timing chain, then carefully undo the bolts holding the sprocket to the end of the camshaft. If locking tab washers are fitted, knock them back with a screwdriver. Try to avoid using too much force when undoing the securing bolts as you risk moving the timing marks out of alignment.

Remove the sprocket, followed by your packing cloth, then use a length of thick string to tie the timing chain up to the bonnet. Make very sure there's no danger of the chain dropping into the sump.

Releasing a timing chain

Pack around the camshaft sprocket with rags then knock back any locking tabs on the sprocket securing bolt (**1**).

Ask a friend to hold the timing chain while you undo the bolt and remove the sprocket (**2**). Finally tie the timing chain up to a convenient point with string (**3**) to prevent it falling into the sump.

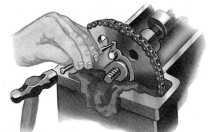

1 If locking tabs are fitted, knock them back with a hammer and screwdriver.

Set the engine timing

Start by removing the cam belt cover (**1**) or the cam cover (**2**) to gain access to the camshaft timing marks. Set the marks so that they align (**3**).

2 Unbolt and remove the cam cover.

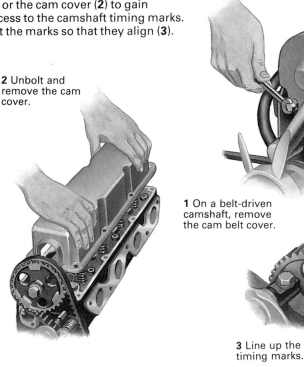

1 On a belt-driven camshaft, remove the cam belt cover.

timing marks

3 Line up the timing marks.

2 Remove the sprocket after undoing its securing bolts.

3 Tie the timing chain out of the way.

With some engines, the camshaft is in the way of some of the cylinder head bolts, so it has to be removed before you can take off the cylinder head. On some Vauxhalls and Volkswagens, the camshaft is contained in its own carrier and the carrier is unbolted.

To remove a camshaft carefully undo the bolts that secure the camshaft bearings, starting from the middle and working round evenly. Once the pressure is off the camshaft, remove it.

To remove a camshaft carrier, progressively loosen the retaining bolts a little at a time, preferably in the sequence shown in your manual. If you do not have a manual, remember that you should undo the bolts in a diagonal sequence, never along one side at a time.

Carefully lift the whole assembly from the head. The cam followers may come out with the carrier or they may remain sitting on top of the valves. If they remain, pick off each one and place it in a jar with that valve's number on – they must be refitted in the same place.

Remove the head

Slacken and then remove the cylinder head bolts in the sequence detailed in your workshop manual. Make a careful note of where each bolt came from as well as any washers, spacers and so on, so that you replace them in the correct order. It's a good idea to stick them through a sheet of cardboard shaped like the cylinder head gasket.

Some cylinder heads are rather heavy and others are awkward to remove because of cramped conditions in the engine compartment. So, wherever possible, ask a friend to help you lift it out.

If you are lucky, the cylinder head will now pull off without any problems, but more often than not it will be a little reluctant because the gasket sticks to the head and block faces.

If this is the case, gently tap the side of the cylinder head with a soft-faced mallet. Be patient when you do this and do not attempt to lever the head off with a screwdriver otherwise you may cause serious –

Removing and refitting the cylinder head

Following the exact sequence given for your car, undo each cylinder head bolt by half a turn each time (**1**) until they are all loose.

With a friend to help, lift off the head (**2**). Fit the new gasket in place (**3**), taking care that any markings are uppermost. Then refit the head and tighten the bolts with a torque wrench.

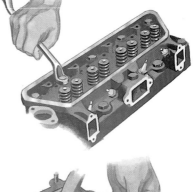

1 Undo the cylinder head bolts a little at a time in sequence.

2 Get a friend to help you lift off the head.

3 Fit the new gasket the right way round on top of the engine block.

and expensive – damage.

On a chain-driven camshaft, lift the head until you can grasp the chain beneath it, then release the string and pull off the head. Tie the string up again.

Once the head is off, carefully check the mating surfaces on both the head and the block for signs of cracks or leaks. Using a steel rule, lay it across the mating surfaces and look along the rule to ensure the surface is flat. If it is not, the head or block will need to be machined by a specialist.

While the head is off, give it a thorough decoke, even if the main purpose of the job is to change the gasket (see pages 31, 32, 33, 34).

Use a flat, stiff, sharp scraper such as an old wood chisel to scrape off all traces of gasket from the faces of both cylinder head and block. Be careful when working on the block not to let any dirt fall into any of the orifices by blocking these with rags.

Refit head

Squirt a little oil on to the tops of the pistons and make sure you have removed all traces of rag. Place the new cylinder head gasket on the block, making sure it is the right

way up – the gasket will be marked 'top' or 'up' (sometimes in the language of your car's manufacturer). A few cars need the gasket smeared with a sealing compound, but check in your workshop manual.

If your cylinder head is held by bolts, it may be difficult to align correctly. If so, place two old pencils in the bolt holes diagonally opposite to use as a guide. They must be longer than the height of the head so they can be removed after fitting.

Refit all the cylinder head bolts or nuts with their washers, then tighten them to the correct torque and in the correct sequence.

Turn the camshaft carefully so that the timing mark on the camshaft sprocket aligns with that on the cylinder head. Reconnect the timing chain or belt taking care not to turn the camshaft at all. Retension the belt, then refit all the covers, manifolds, carburettor etc.

When restarting the engine, allow it to warm up and check for leaks from the cylinder head gasket, cam cover gasket, coolant hoses and exhaust. After 500 miles (800km), recheck and adjust the tightness of the cylinder head bolts as the head normally settles a bit during the initial period after overhaul.

Decoking your engine

Whenever you remove the cylinder head to replace a damaged inlet or exhaust valve, it pays to give the head a thorough cleaning. This is known as decoking or decarbonizing. Not only does it help to make the engine run more smoothly and economically, it can also improve engine performance. (Most modern engines no longer need a regular, frequent decoke in the way that much earlier engines used to.)

Preparation

Begin by unbolting the inlet and exhaust manifolds from the cylinder head. The nuts or bolts are usually accessible, though a few of them may require a socket and slim extension bar or box spanner to undo. Also take off the temperature sensor to avoid damaging it.

You might like to leave the spark plugs in the cylinder head for now, as they will protect the plug hole threads from filling with loose

carbon when you clean the combustion chambers. It is worth buying and fitting a new set for when you rebuild the head.

Remove valves

To remove the valves, you will need a special tool called a valve spring compressor. This compresses and so shortens the valve springs so that the valve-retaining collets (also called cotters) can be removed.

The type of compressor you need varies depending on whether your car has an overhead valve or an overhead cam engine. The one covered on this sheet is for an overhead valve engine. For an overhead cam engine, you may need a special long- or angled-reach compressor to clear the camshaft carriers – ask when you hire or buy.

Lay the cylinder head on blocks of wood so that it is clear of your working surface. Tip it on to one

 **advanced**

Tools and materials

☐ Spanners, sockets and screwdrivers
☐ Valve spring compressor
☐ Blocks of wood
☐ Hammer
☐ Containers for valves
☐ Electric drill and wire brushes
☐ Goggles
☐ Scraper tools (see text)
☐ Valve grinding tool
☐ Grinding paste
☐ New valve stem oil seals
☐ New valves (if required)
☐ Clean engine oil

collets

valve spring

retaining cap

Retaining parts

The valve spring fits around the valve stem and is topped by the retaining cap. The cap is locked on to the valve stem by the tapered collets.

☆ Storing valve parts

Before you remove the valves, find a separate container for each one so that you can store the parts for each valve away from the others – it is important that you do not muddle up the parts for different valves.

Mark each box with its valve number (1 to 8 on a four cylinder engine, numbering from the front backwards). Then, when you have finished decoking and have reassembled the valves, you can be sure of replacing them in exactly the same order.

Working on the head

Support the cylinder head on wooden blocks to protect the casting from damage. You will need to

unbolt external parts such as the manifolds and the thermostat housing to avoid damaging them.

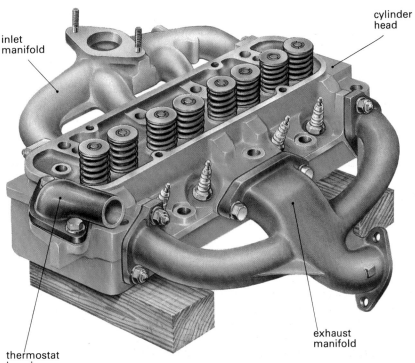

inlet manifold

cylinder head

thermostat housing

exhaust manifold

Removing the inlet and exhaust valves

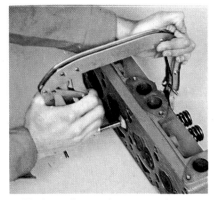

1 Fit the valve spring compressor over the cylinder head so that the forked end fits over the valve cap and the cup end bears against the valve head.

2 Compress the valve spring by operating the handle or the T-bar on the compressor tool. Keep going until you can remove the split collets from the retaining cap.

3 Carefully release the compressor tool until the valve spring is no longer under tension. Then pull off the valve retaining cap from the valve spring.

4 Lift the valve spring from over the valve stem. Most cars have a single spring (as here) but a few have two – one fitted inside the other.

5 The oil seal fits around the valve stem. Some cars have seals fitted only to the inlet valves, others have them on both inlet and exhaust. Prise or pull off the seal.

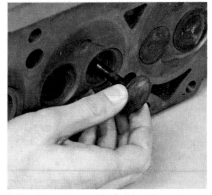

6 Push on the end of the valve stem so that the valve head pops out into the combustion chamber. Use fingers to pull out the valve – it may need a firm tug to remove.

side and fit the valve spring compressor. The forked end must fit over the top cap or collar of the valve spring, and the screw end with the T-handle must bear on the head of the valve inside the combustion chamber.

Turn the T-handle or squeeze the press-handle of the tool so that the valve spring is compressed. You may find that the split collets won't release their hold. If so, cover the head of the valve spring with a cloth, and tap the spring with a hammer. This should jolt the collets loose.

Pull each collet out of the top of the valve spring retaining cap – take care not to drop them as they are easily lost. Gently release the tension on the tool by unwinding

the T-handle. Lift off the cap, followed by the valve spring. On some cars there may be two valve springs fitted to each valve.

Now push on the end of the valve stem so that the head of the valve pops out into the combustion chamber. Pull the valve right out – it may need a hefty tug. Watch out for any oil seals around the valve stem. Remove the other valves in the same way, storing all the components in labelled containers (see sideline, previous page).

Decoke the head

How you decoke the cylinder head depends on what it is made of. Cast-iron heads can be cleaned with a wire brush fitted in an electric

drill. Special small tapered brushes are available for decoking. They allow you to work right into every nook and cranny.

Do not use a wire brush to clean up an aluminium cylinder head – it may severely damage the soft metal. Instead, soak the head in paraffin to soften the carbon deposits, then scrape them off with a soft copper brush or a hardwood or plastic scraper.

Clean chambers

Start by cleaning all traces of carbon from the combustion chambers in the cylinder head. Work right into all the corners. If you have removed the spark plugs, be very careful when cleaning round the spark plug hole, or you may damage the threads.

Once all the combustion chambers are clean and shiny, use the wire brush to clean out the inlet and exhaust ports. Work through the valve holes and the inlet and exhaust port holes. Any really stubborn deposits can be removed by scratching them off carefully with a blunt screwdriver.

Remove all traces of carbon particles from the ports and the combustion chamber, using the cooling air from your drill or a foot pump. Clean the flat face of the cylinder head to remove all traces of old gasket.

Modern gaskets have a resin coating that sticks the gasket to the surface, making it difficult to remove. Use the smooth side of an old hacksaw blade or a paint scraper to remove traces of gasket and resin from a cast-iron cylinder head. On an alloy head use a hardwood scraper. Take care not to scratch the surface when you do this.

Valve cleaning

The carbon must also be scraped off the valves. Mount the valve in the chuck of your drill, then switch the drill on. Use a screwdriver to remove the carbon from the spinning valve – wear goggles to protect your eyes when doing this. If necessary, take off any remaining deposits with fine emery cloth.

Inspect parts

Check each valve for wear around the bevelled edge that sits in the cylinder head. A little light pitting can be easily ground out, but if a chunk of valve is missing, or the surface is badly pitted, you need a new valve.

Also check where the valve seats in the cylinder head. Again the bevelled edge must be sound and only lightly pitted. If you find damage more serious than this you should seek advice from a garage or engine rebuilder.

Valve grinding

If the valves are good enough to be reused, they must be ground or 'lapped' to match their seats in the cylinder head. This will help to ensure a gas-tight seal and good compression. If you are fitting new valves, find out from your dealer whether the valves have to be ground in (see sideline overleaf).

Smear a little engine oil on to the

Decoking the pistons

As well as the head and valves, you should also decoke the pistons, and remove traces of cylinder head gasket from the cylinder block.

Before you start, plug all the water and oil passages in the engine with wads of cloth. This prevents carbon particles falling into them. You should also plug the gap between the cylinders and the cores to prevent dirt falling in. Do this by running a smear of grease around the edge of each piston.

Use a wooden scraper (as above), or carefully use your drill and decoking wire brush, to take off almost all the carbon from the top of each piston. Leave a ¼in (6mm) ring of carbon around the edge of each piston – if you don't the engine's oil consumption may increase until the ring of carbon forms again. Use a fine emery cloth to polish each piston to a high gloss, then remove all loose carbon with a vacuum cleaner.

Turn the engine to move each piston down in its cylinder, then wipe off the grease complete with the dirt. Wipe the pistons, cylinder bores and the flat surface of the cylinder block clean with a paraffin-soaked rag. Dry them off with a non-fluffy rag. Finally smear each cylinder bore with clean engine oil. Remove the wads of cloth from the oil and water passages.

Decoking the cylinder head and valves

Using your electric drill and a special decoking wire brush, clean out all traces of carbon from the inlet and exhaust ports (**1**).

Do the same with the combustion chamber (**2**).

To clean the valves, mount each one in the chuck of your drill, then use a screwdriver to scrape off the carbon (**3**).

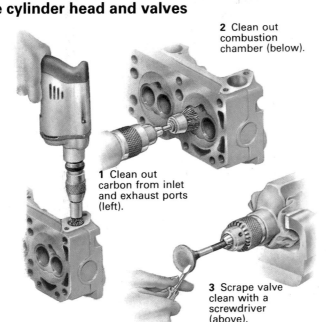

2 Clean out combustion chamber (below).

1 Clean out carbon from inlet and exhaust ports (left).

3 Scrape valve clean with a screwdriver (above).

⚠️ No grinding

On several engines, the new valves have a thin coating which resists erosion or burning by hot gases. This must not be removed, so you should not grind the valves into the cylinder head. Ask your dealer if your engine has this type of valve.

If the valve seats in the head need grinding, use one of the old valves to do it.

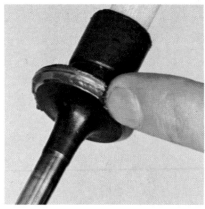

Grinding paste

Grinding the valves is done by smearing a little paste containing carborundum particles on the bevelled edge of the valve (above). The valve is then inserted into its seat and rotated from side to side using a valve grinding tool. This tool is simply a wooden shaft with a rubber sucker on one end. The sucker sticks to the head of the valve.

As you rotate the tool and valve, the paste gradually removes any imperfections on the taper of both valve and seat, so that they eventually match perfectly. Be careful not to grind too hard, or you may damage the valve by removing too much metal.

Grinding paste comes in two grades – coarse for removing deep pitting and fine for finishing off or grinding in new valves. Neither of these grades can be used to cure severe damage, which must be done by a garage or engine specialist.

Grinding the valves

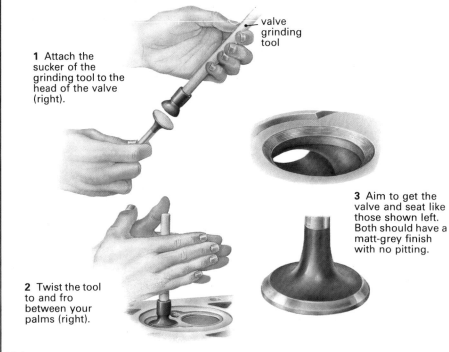

1 Attach the sucker of the grinding tool to the head of the valve (right).

valve grinding tool

2 Twist the tool to and fro between your palms (right).

3 Aim to get the valve and seat like those shown left. Both should have a matt-grey finish with no pitting.

Take care not to grind off too much metal. Keep the newly formed seating narrow – avoid grinding a

valve stem, then smear a small amount of coarse grinding paste on to the bevelled edge of the valve. If you are grinding in a new valve, use only fine paste. Stick the sucker of your grinding tool on to the head of the valve. Insert the valve into its guide then briskly rotate the grinding tool back and forth between your palms, pressing down at the same time.

After a minute of continuous grinding, lift the tool up to raise the valve off its seat, turn it through 45 degrees and continue grinding for another minute. This redistributes the paste and ensures even grinding.

Take the valve out, wipe the paste off both it and the seat, and check that the pitting has gone. If not, apply more paste and carry on. Once the worst of the pitting is removed, switch to fine paste and carry on grinding until the valve and the seat have an unbroken matt-grey finish all the way round.

If the pitting cannot be removed, then you must fit a new valve or, if the damage is to the cylinder head, have the valve seats recut by an engine rebuilder.

step in the bevel-edged face of the head. The valve seat should be a matt-grey all over.

Do the other valves in the same way. Use paraffin to remove all traces of grinding paste from the valves and cylinder head, then leave it to dry.

Refitting valves

Smear each valve stem with clean oil, then refit it to the cylinder head. If oil seals are fitted, you need to use new ones. Slip the new seal over the valve stem taking care not to damage the lips. Fit the valve spring or springs over the valve stem, with the retaining cap on top. Fit the compressor, and use it to compress the spring. Keep compressing until you can fit the two collets into the cap. Slowly release the compressor, making sure that the raised lips on the collets engage with the grooves in the valve stem.

Remove the compressor tool, and refit the other valves in the same way. Give each valve stem a sharp tap with a hammer to ensure that all the collets are firmly seated. Then refit all the parts you removed earlier. The cylinder head is now ready for refitting.

Adjusting a camshaft timing belt

The toothed rubber drive belt that drives the camshaft on an overhead cam (OHC) engine must be properly tensioned to operate correctly and quietly. Most manufacturers recommend checking the belt tension at every service, and also checking the belt for wear. Even if the belt isn't damaged it should be replaced every 36,000 miles (60,000km) •or when specified by the manufacturer. If the belt should break, the valves and the pistons will meet, causing serious damage to the engine.

Special tools

Some cars, such as Fords, need a special tool to slacken off the adjuster. The tools can usually be bought at a dealer's spares department, or at accessory shops if the car is a popular model.

Get at the belt

Before you can adjust the belt, you first have to get access to it. The belt is covered by a steel or plastic

advanced

Tools and materials
☐ Spanners and sockets
☐ Screwdrivers
☐ Hammer and block of wood
☐ Bucket
☐ Special adjusting tool, if necessary
☐ Spring balance, if necessary

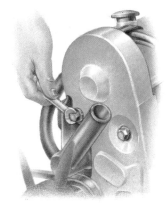

Removing the cover
Undo all the bolts holding the cover to the engine and lift the cover off. Some bolts may be well hidden near the bottom – make sure you remove them all.

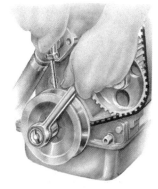

Removing the pulley
On some Vauxhalls the cover will not come off without removing the crankshaft pulley. Use a screwdriver to lock the engine in position, then undo the nut or bolt holding on the crankshaft pulley. Lever the pulley off using two large screwdrivers or a special puller tool.

Ford OHC cam belt
On the Ford Pinto engine the belt is tensioned by a spring-loaded wheel mounted on a metal plate. The plate is bolted to the engine and is pivoted to adjust the tension.

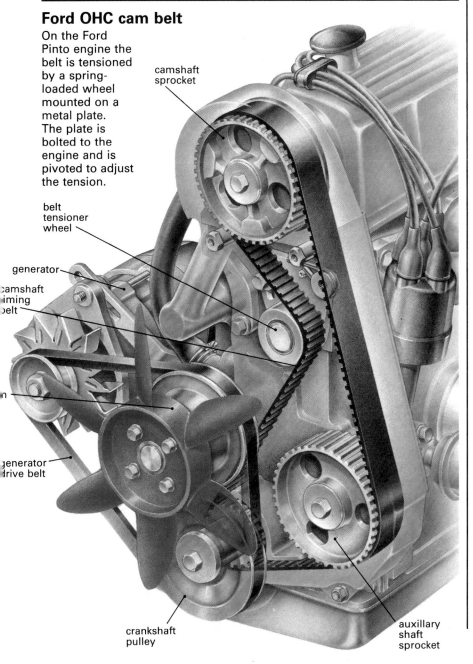

camshaft sprocket

belt tensioner wheel

generator

camshaft timing belt

generator drive belt

crankshaft pulley

auxillary shaft sprocket

☆ Checking the belt

While you are tensioning the belt, give it a thorough inspection for signs of cracking or oil contamination. Look very closely for cracks since they may be quite fine and difficult to spot. Check especially on the inner edge where the drive teeth are.

Don't forget to examine the whole length by turning the engine over. If there is any sign of damage you will have to fit a new belt.

cover, bolted to the front of the engine. On most cars some parts have to be taken off before you can remove the cover.

Start by removing the generator drive belt. Slacken the bolts holding the generator to the engine, and then ease off the belt. On some cars you will also need to remove the cooling fan and the water pump pulley. Undo the bolts holding them to the water pump and lift them off.

You may also find that the top radiator hose is in the way. If so, partly drain the cooling system, then undo the clips at each end of the hose and pull it off.

Usually the belt can be adjusted with the crankshaft pulley still fitted, but often the cover goes around the pulley so you may have to take it off (see sideline). On some Hondas there is an engine mounting in the way of the cover, so you have to jack up the engine and take off the mounting.

Remove the cover

Once everything is out of the way you can unbolt the belt cover. Check the cover all over for bolts and undo them. Make a note of which bolts go where as they may be of different lengths. Look out for any bolts

hidden at the bottom of the cover as they are often recessed. On Vauxhalls there is an extra self-tapping screw at the top right-hand rear of the cover. On Volkswagens there are several bolts fitted through from the rear of the belt cover.

With all the bolts out, pull the belt cover clear. If it is stuck, gently tap it with a hammer and block of wood to jar it free. If it still doesn't come loose, check again in case you have missed a hidden bolt.

With the cover off you can see the whole of the belt and the tensioner wheel (where fitted). On Volkswagens you can see the bolts holding the water pump.

Tensioners

Some cars, such as Fords with the Pinto engine, are fitted with a spring-loaded tensioner, which automatically tensions the camshaft timing belt when you release the bolts locking it in position. If there is no automatic spring loading, you have to check the tension by hand and then tighten the tensioner bolts while keeping the belt tensioned.

Now turn to the appropriate section for your car to find out how to check and, if necessary, adjust the tension.

Tensioning a Ford cam belt

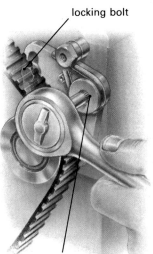

locking bolt

pivot-spring bolt

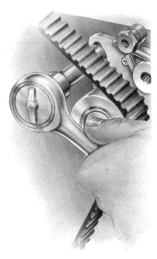

1 Look at the tensioner, and find the two bolts shown above. Slacken the locking bolt with a socket or spanner. Loosen the special pivot-spring bolt using the special splined tool.

2 Releasing the bolts allows the spring-loaded tensioner to move harder against the belt. To even out the tension, use a spanner or socket to turn the engine two full turns clockwise.

3 Now tighten the tensioner locking bolt with a socket or spanner. Use the special splined tool and a torque wrench to tighten the pivot-spring bolt to a torque of 14lb ft.

Tensioning a Leyland O-series cam belt

The belt tensioner on the O-series engine is not spring-loaded, and you have to tension the belt in much the same way as you would a generator drive belt.

To measure the tension, you need a spring balance together with an L-shaped hook which will sit flat against the belt – if necessary make one out of a metal coathanger. The balance must be able to measure at least 13lb (6kg).

Fit the L-shaped hook to the belt midway between the camshaft and crankshaft sprockets – level with the intake pipe of the water pump. Ensure that the hook sits squarely between two teeth on the belt. Attach the spring balance to the other end of the hook, and pull on the belt until it is level with the raised marker on the water pump intake pipe. Note the reading on the spring balance.

The reading should be about 11lb (5kg) for a used belt, and 13lb (6kg) for a new one. If the reading is not correct you must adjust the belt tension.

The tensioner wheel is held by two bolts. Loosen them both just enough to let the tensioner slide, then lever the tensioner harder against the belt to tighten it, or away from it to

loosen. Lock the tensioner with the bolt which fits through the slot, then recheck the tension. If it is correct, tighten both bolts – if not, readjust. Refit the belt cover and the generator drive belt not forgetting to tension it.

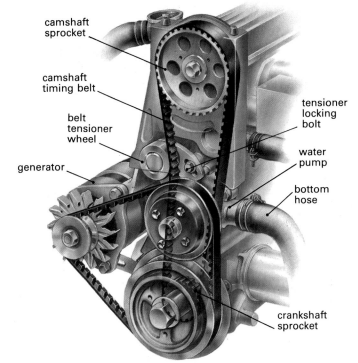

camshaft sprocket

camshaft timing belt

belt tensioner wheel

generator

tensioner locking bolt

water pump

bottom hose

crankshaft sprocket

On the O-series engine, the tensioner is not spring-loaded, so you have to check the belt tension using a spring balance.

The tensioner consists of a wheel fitted to a plate that pivots on the engine block (above).

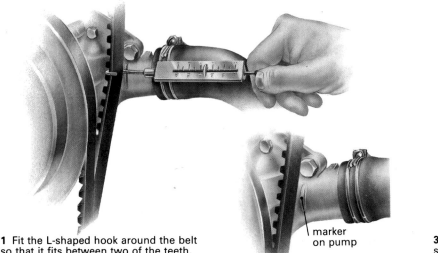

1 Fit the L-shaped hook around the belt so that it fits between two of the teeth. Make sure you are pulling close to the point where the belt passes the water pump intake pipe.

marker on pump

2 Pull the belt out until it aligns with the marker and take a reading from the spring balance.

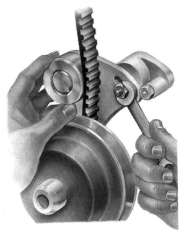

3 If the reading is more or less than it should be, slacken both the tensioner lock bolts, and move the tensioner towards the belt to tighten, and away to loosen – recheck the tension.

Tensioning some Opel and Vauxhall cam belts

No spring is fitted to the tensioner on these overhead cam engines, so you have to check and adjust the belt tension by hand. To check the tension, grasp the belt midway along the longest straight run between two sprockets, and try to twist it sideways.

If the belt tension is correct, you will be able to twist the belt through 90° – no more and no less.

If the tension is wrong, slacken both the pivot and locking bolts on the tensioner until it is free to move. Slide the tensioner clockwise to increase the belt tension, anticlockwise to reduce it. Tighten the tensioner nut again, and recheck the tension. Adjust if necessary.

Refit the belt cover tightening all the nuts and the self-tapping screw in the top right-hand rear side of the cover. Also refit the crankshaft pulley and do it up to the correct torque. Refit the fan and water pump pulley and the generator drive belt, and retension the drive belt.

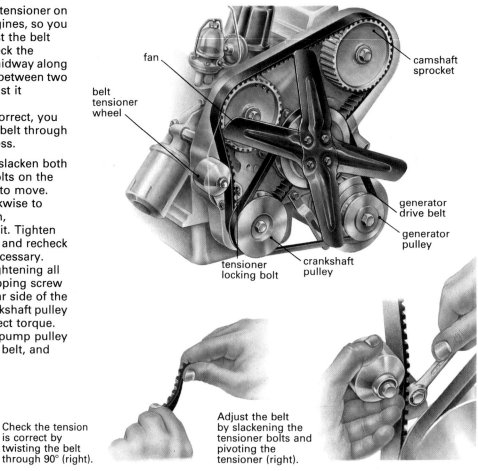

fan

belt tensioner wheel

camshaft sprocket

generator drive belt

generator pulley

tensioner locking bolt

crankshaft pulley

Check the tension is correct by twisting the belt through 90° (right).

Adjust the belt by slackening the tensioner bolts and pivoting the tensioner (right).

Tensioning a Volkswagen cam belt

With the cover off, you will be able to see the belt running around the crankshaft and camshaft sprockets and around the water pump. The belt is tensioned by altering the position of the water pump.

To check the tension, twist the belt through 90° at the midpoint of its longest run. If you can twist it through more or less than 90° it needs adjusting.

If the tension is wrong slacken off the bolts holding the water pump to the engine, then use a screwdriver to lever the pump away from the engine block. The pump will rotate around the three bolts, sliding on slots in its body. Turn the pump until the tension is correct and, while holding the pump in position, do up the water pump bolts.

Refit the timing belt cover, fitting the bolts from the front and rear of the cover as necessary. Refit and tension the generator drive belt.

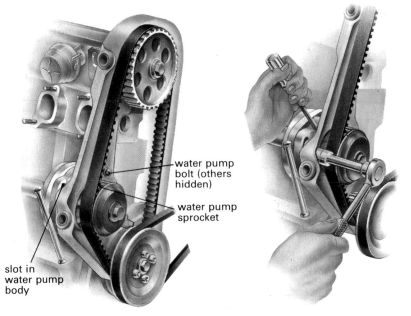

water pump bolt (others hidden)

water pump sprocket

slot in water pump body

On some Volkswagens the belt runs around a sprocket on the water pump. To adjust the belt, loosen the bolts holding the water pump, then use a screwdriver to lever the pump around. Retighten the bolts when the tension is correct.

Replacing the engine mountings

bracket from mounting to engine | rubber mounting | mounting point on bodywork

Engine mountings for rear-wheel drive

Tools and materials
☐ New engine mountings
☐ Screwdrivers
☐ Spanners or sockets
☐ Jack and block of wood
☐ Rag

The engine mountings are rubber blocks bonded (glued) to metal plates fitted between the engine and the bodywork. They act as a vibration and noise absorber between the engine and the passenger compartment. They also allow the engine (and gearbox) to move slightly to compensate for bumps in the road and engine torque, so preventing any part of the engine and the bodyshell being subjected to undue stress.

The mountings can crack, whether through oil contamination or just old age. The bonding may also fail, allowing the rubber to peel away from the metal plates.

Checking for damage

The first sign that an engine mounting is failing is usually an increase in vibration from the engine, or a loud thumping sound as some part of the engine, exhaust or transmission moves far enough to hit the bodywork.

☆ Stabilizer bars

If your engine is held steady by a stabilizer bar (also called a tie-bar or steady bar), you may have to unbolt it so that the engine can be lifted high enough to remove the engine mounting.

In most cases the bar is simply bolted to the engine and to the body at each end. Using a spanner or socket, undo the bolts and any brackets (see above), and carefully prise the bar clear.

When refitting the bar, leave the bolts loose until you have run the engine. This ensures that the bushes in the bar are not stressed. After running the engine do the bolts up tight.

Bobbin mounting

A common type of engine mounting is the bobbin mounting, shown here and above. It consists of a rubber block, with a steel plate bonded to each end. Sticking out of each plate is a threaded stud, one bolted to a bracket on the engine, the other to a bracket on the car's bodywork.

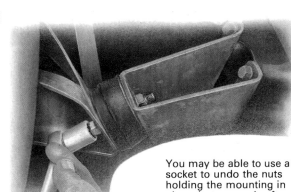

You may be able to use a socket to undo the nuts holding the mounting in place, but access is often difficult.

Lift the bonnet and look for the mountings. On rear-wheel drive cars they are easily seen. There are usually two, one at each side of the engine.

With transverse engine, front-wheel drive cars, there may be up to four mountings, often tucked away underneath the engine and not so easy to spot.

Check each mounting for signs of splitting, cracking or peeling – use a screwdriver to lever the mounting, as some cracks may not show up with the engine at rest. If the mountings appear to be sound, start the engine and ask a friend to rev it up for a moment.

As the speed rises, watch the mountings. They should flex a little but not allow the engine to move more than about 1in (25mm). If the engine visibly rocks about, and parts of it hit the bodywork, then the mountings have probably become soft.

However, if the engine has a stabilizer bar (also called a tie-bar – see sideline, previous page) then check the bushes in it as they are prone to wearing out.

If you find a damaged or soft mounting, you must fit new ones all round. This may seem unnecessary but it is advisable because, if you fit just a single mounting, it will be stiffer than the old ones. This imposes stresses on the older mountings which may then crack.

Support the engine

To remove the mountings, you have to jack up and support the engine. There is usually no need to raise the car on ramps or stands except on some front-wheel drive models.

Place your jack under the engine sump, spreading the load with a block of wood roughly 1in (25mm) thick. Jack up slowly until the weight of the engine has been taken off the mountings. Take care not to raise the jack too far or you may strain the cooling hoses or exhaust pipe. Unbolt the stabilizer bar if your car is fitted with one.

Change the mountings

Replace the mountings one at a time to avoid accidents. Undo the nuts or bolts holding the mounting to the engine. On some cars you may have to take off the metal bracket that runs between mounting and engine block before the mounting can be removed. Lift the old mounting off, clean up the area where it fits, then drop the new mounting in. Refit the nuts and bolts, but don't fully tighten them just yet.

Fit the other mountings, then slowly lower the jack until the full weight is taken on the mountings. Reconnect any stabilizer bars that are fitted, then start the engine and allow it to run for a few minutes to let it settle down on the mountings. Stop the engine and fully tighten all the nuts and bolts.

Renewing the engine mountings

1 Support the engine with a jack, using a flat piece of wood to spread the load.

2 Undo the nuts or bolts holding the mounting's bracket to the engine.

3 Remove the bracket from its mounting.

4 Remove the old mounting (below).

First place a jack under the engine sump, with a piece of wood between the two to spread the load (**1**). If you cannot get at the mountings with the car on the ground, raise it up on ramps or stands.

Lift the engine until the mountings are no longer under load, then undo all the nuts and bolts holding the mounting or its bracket to the engine (**2**). Lift the bracket clear of the mounting (**3**), then release the nuts or bolts securing the mounting to the bodywork or the sub-frame. These are often inaccessible but you should be able to reach in with a spanner. Lift the old mounting off (**4**).

Fit the new mounting and the fixing but leave them loose. Lower the jack, run the engine to settle the mountings, then switch off and tighten all fixings.

40

Checking and renewing engine dampers

Some engines are prone to rocking on their rubber mountings, particularly at idling speed, and so are fitted with a telescopic hydraulic damper and/or a tie-bar.

A telescopic damper is a miniature version of the damper found on many suspension systems. It is usually mounted between a bracket attached to the cylinder head or engine block and another bracket attached to the body structure in the engine bay. Its role is to dampen engine vibrations and restrict the engine's rocking movement.

The engine may also have a tie-bar, either in conjunction with the damper or on its own. This is simply a plain bar with a bushed eye at each end, one end being bolted to the engine and the other to the bodywork.

Damper check

You should check the damper at the major service intervals; every 12,000 miles (20,000km) or one year. But do this sooner if you suspect they may be faulty, for example if you hear a thumping noise from the engine when you accelerate or

Tools and materials
☐ Spanners
☐ Vice
☐ Rags
☐ Stout screwdriver
☐ New damper or tie-bar parts as needed
☐ Washing-up liquid for lubricating

Tie-bar or damper?

Some car engines are fitted with a tie-bar, others with a damper. Some may have both, others none. To find out which, if any, your car has, look around the side of the engine. A tie-bar (below) is a simple rigid metal bar, with bushed eyes at each end, attached to brackets to link the engine to the car bodywork. A damper (bottom) resembles a small telescopic suspension damper with a bracket at each end.

damper — vice

Testing an engine damper

Place the damper upright in a vice and push it down and then up to compress it and lengthen it. It should give an even amount of resistance throughout the length of its travel and in both directions.

If it offers hardly any resistance or if you can hardly move it at all, or if it is stiffer in one direction than the other, it is worn and you will have to replace the whole unit. You cannot buy parts for it.

If you don't have a vice, you can easily carry out this test by squeezing and extending the damper with your hands.

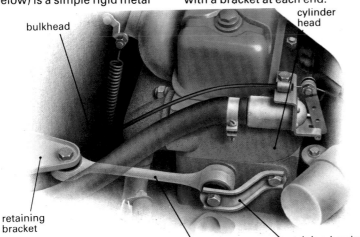
bulkhead
cylinder head
retaining bracket
retaining bracket
tie-bar

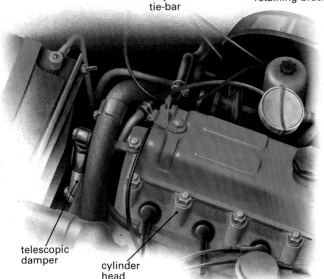
telescopic damper
cylinder head

Adjustable tie-bars

On some cars, the length of the tie-bar can be adjusted to minimize the strain on the engine. But if the bar is set too long or too short, this will strain the rubber bushes and eventually cause them to fail.

Some bars can be adjusted simply by undoing a locknut (**1**) and then turning the bar so that it screws into or out of its sleeve to adjust its length (**2**). Other tie-bars have to be adjusted by unbolting them at one end and then screwing them into or out of the sleeve.

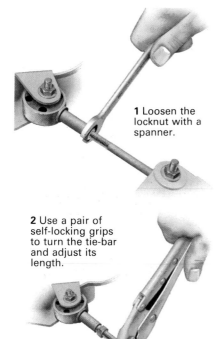

1 Loosen the locknut with a spanner.

2 Use a pair of self-locking grips to turn the tie-bar and adjust its length.

To adjust the length of the tie-bar, use a pair of self-locking pliers to screw it outwards until it starts to push against the engine. Then screw it inwards – this time counting the number of turns – until it just starts to pull the engine in the opposite direction.

Now screw the tie-bar back again half this number of turns. It should now be at its correct length.

Your service manual may give a maximum and a minimum length for the tie-bar. If so, check its actual length against these figures. If it falls outside this range, the engine mountings may have distorted or perished. Check them as on pages 39, 40.

Checking a tie-bar

With the tie-bar in place, use a stout screwdriver to try to lever the bar against its mountings (**1**). If there is any movement one of its bushes has probably worn. To replace it, unbolt the bar from its brackets (**2**) and prise out the faulty bush. The new bush should push in easily (**3**), but if not lubricate it with a little washing-up liquid.

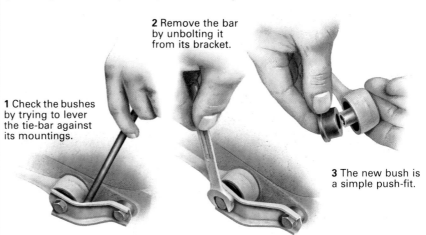

2 Remove the bar by unbolting it from its bracket.

1 Check the bushes by trying to lever the tie-bar against its mountings.

3 The new bush is a simple push-fit.

brake, sometimes accompanied by excessive movement of the gear lever. Another symptom is severe juddering when letting up the clutch in first or reverse.

The damper is attached to its mounting points by bushed eyes. Examine the rubber bushes for cracks, splits, oil contamination, swelling and perishing. If you see any, you usually have to replace the whole damper unit.

Also examine the damper for signs of leaking. If you see any – or if you don't but you still suspect it is faulty – unbolt it from the engine and test it in a vice (see sideline, previous page).

Tie-bar check

You should check the tie-bar at the same interval as you would a damper, or as soon as you suspect it may be failing. The symptoms of a failed tie-bar are the same as for a failed engine damper.

To check a tie-bar, first wipe it and its mountings clean with a rag. Examine the bushes at each end for distortion, softness, cracking, perishing or oil contamination. Try to move the bar by hand or with a lever such as a stout screwdriver. If there is any movement at all, one or both bushes may be faulty.

To replace the bushes, unbolt both ends of the tie-bar from its mountings and remove it. Inspect the bar, its bolts and its mounting points for damage and rust.

On some cars, the bushes are integral with the tie-bar and you have to replace the whole bar rather than just the bushes themselves. On most cars, however, you can simply prise the old bushes out of their eyes and push-fit new ones in place.

Early Minis have a metal cone which fits inside the bush. Fit the new bush to the eye, then position the cone and the bushed eye in a vice and tighten up the jaws so that the cone is forced into the eye.

When refitting the bar, you may need to lever it into position while you tighten the bolts. It helps to have a friend hold the bar in place while you do this.

Mountings check

Once you have replaced the damper or tie-bar, check the engine mountings. These may have suffered from excessive wear caused by the faulty damper or tie-bar.

Examine the rubber bushes in the mountings for signs of cracks, perishing or softening, and look at the rubber-to-metal bond to see if the rubber has started to separate from the metal there. If you see any signs of damage, replace the engine mountings, following the steps given on pages 39, 40. It's best to fit new mountings all round.

Tracing an oil leak from the engine

Where to look for leaks

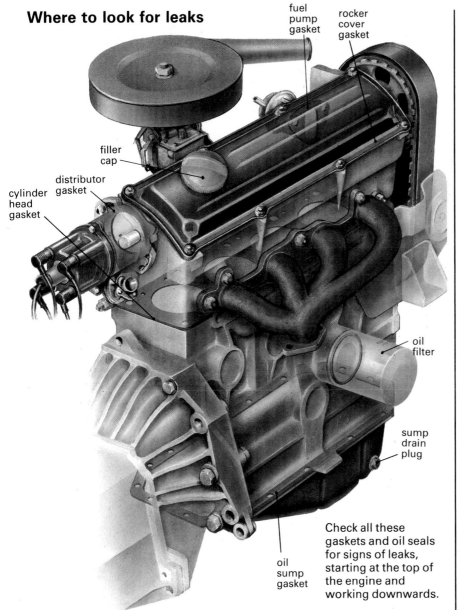

fuel pump gasket

rocker cover gasket

filler cap

distributor gasket

cylinder head gasket

oil filter

sump drain plug

oil sump gasket

Check all these gaskets and oil seals for signs of leaks, starting at the top of the engine and working downwards.

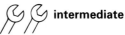
Tools and materials
☐ Degreasing fluid and paint brush
☐ Plastic bags
☐ Hose
☐ Mirror and torch for inspection
☐ Screwdrivers and spanners
☐ New gaskets and oil seals as needed
☐ New washers and other parts as needed
☐ New engine oil

☆ Testing with a mirror
The oil may be leaking from an area hidden deep in the engine bay. Use a small mirror to inspect these areas, but be careful because you will probably need to have the engine running while you do this.

☆ Clean the engine
You will find it much easier to discover the source of the leak if you first clean the engine thoroughly with a paint brush and an engine degreasing agent. Protect all electrical parts with plastic bags held in place with sticky tape. Then hose away the degreaser with water.

If your engine is very dirty, you may prefer to take it to a garage to be steam cleaned.

If your engine oil needs topping up more than usual, or if you see a pool of oil under your car after it has been standing for a while, then your engine has an oil leak. You need to trace the source of the leak – which will probably be from a gasket or an oil seal – immediately, otherwise the engine could be seriously damaged.

The best way to find the source of a leak is to systematically examine all the engine's gaskets and oil seals, starting at the top of the engine and working down.

Rocker cover

Run the engine so that the moving parts beneath the rocker or cam-shaft cover are spraying oil around the inside. This highlights the leak.

Look carefully for oil seeping out from around the cover flange, par-ticularly at the front and rear ends where the gasket may not be seal-ing properly. The leak is probably due either to a broken or distorted gasket, or to uneven or overtight-ened cover screws.

Check the side of the gasket in

the area around the leak. (Use a mirror if it is hidden by the rim of the cover.) If the gasket looks broken you should replace it. If it is distorted or displaced, you can reposition it as a temporary repair, though you should fit a new one as soon as possible.

When you have straightened or replaced the gasket, tighten up the cover screws just enough to press the cover firmly on to the gasket, but no more – overtightening will distort the cover and the gasket and cause more leaks.

If you can find no flaw in the gasket, it may be that the rocker cover is too tight. Loosen the screws and, as above, tighten them up again so that the cover just nips the gasket but no more.

If the rocker cover is secured by nuts and bolts, the leak may be caused by a wrongly fitted sealing washer just under the fixing or by the nuts not being tight enough. Check the condition of the washers and the tightness of the nuts close to the source of the leak. If in doubt, fit new washers.

Check the rubber or cork gasket on the oil filler cap too; it may have perished. The final possibility is that the cover itself has been warped by overtightening. If so, it will probably need replacing.

Head gasket

Again with the engine running, check for oil leaks at the cylinder head gasket. If there is a leak, this means that the rocker shaft or the camshaft oil supply passage is leaking at the point where it passes through the head gasket.

You can try tightening the cylinder head fixing just a little to see if that cures the problem. If it doesn't, then the head gasket has broken or become distorted, or the face of the cylinder head or the cylinder block (where they meet each other) has become distorted or cracked. These problems are best tackled by a garage.

Distributor flange

With the engine running, check carefully for leaks around the mounting flange where the distributor is attached to the camshaft cover

Tracking down the leak

1 Rocker or camshaft cover Check these gaskets for leaks. Some rocker or camshaft cover gaskets are held in place by small tongues. Position them properly before tightening the cover (top). Tighten all nuts and bolts evenly (above) and take care not to overtighten.

2 Distributor flange The distributor will be mounted to the engine either on the camshaft cover (top) or on the crankcase (above). Check the tightness of the mounting and the condition of the gasket or O-ring oil seal, whichever is fitted.

3 Crankcase side cover Tighten the bolt to compress the gasket (above). This may stop the leak.

4 Fuel pump mounting A mechanical fuel pump (above) may leak where it mounts to the engine block.

or the crankcase. On some engines this mounting is sealed by a thin gasket; on others there is an O-ring rubber oil seal.

If there is a leak, these parts need replacing, for which you have to take off the distributor.

Side covers

Some engines, such as those fitted to certain BL and Chrysler cars, have one or more covers over the camshaft tappet chamber. They are on the side of the crankcase about halfway up the engine and are called side covers.

The covers are hidden by the inlet and exhaust manifolds, so leaks are difficult to spot. Have the engine running, and use a mirror and a torch to try to spot oil running down from the lower edge of each cover. If you see any, try tightening the securing bolt or bolts. If this fails to cure it, you need to replace the gasket.

Fuel pump mounting

Only mechanical fuel pumps, mounted on the engine, can develop a leak. With the engine running, check for signs of oil leaking from

Check the dipstick
Look for signs of oil leaking past the top of the dipstick. If you see any, replace the O-ring round the dipstick (where one is fitted). It usually pulls straight off, and the new one pushes on in its place. Lubricate the new O-ring with clean engine oil before fitting.

5 Timing cover A leaking oil seal here usually means that oil has been sprayed out to other parts of the engine bay by the pulley wheel (above). Check for signs of this.

6 Crankshaft rear seal Look for signs of oil leaking down between the clutch housing and the sump (above). The cause is probably a leaking crankshaft rear oil seal. To fit a new seal you need to take out either the engine or the gearbox; you may prefer to get a garage to do this.

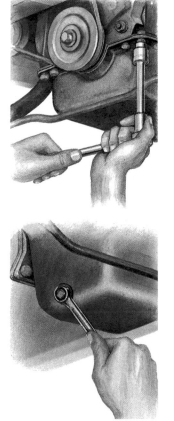

7 Sump pan Tighten all the bolts holding the sump pan to the engine (top), but do not overtighten in case you distort the gasket. If this fails to cure the leak, fit a new gasket – there may be more than one.

If the sump plug is leaking, make sure it is fitted correctly and tighten it with a spanner (above). Replace the plug washer if it is damaged.

Ford oil pump adapter
Some cars, such as Fords with a Kent engine, have an oil pump adapter between the oil filter and the engine. To check this adapter for leaks you will probably need to raise the front of the car on ramps – don't forget to chock the rear wheels and apply the handbrake.

If there is a leak, you will see oil streaming from the oil filter seal or the pump adapter housing because the oil is under more pressure here than elsewhere in the system. Replace the gasket if the leak is serious; slight seepage can sometimes be cured by checking the tightness of the fixings (above).

the underside of the pump mounting flange or gasket.

If you see any, first check that the pump mounting nuts are not loose – if they are, take care not to overtighten them. If the leak persists, fit a new gasket after first smearing it with a non-setting sealant and making sure that both the pump flange face and the mounting face are clean.

On many engines the two faces are separated, not by a single gasket, but by a thick spacer plate sandwiched between two thin paper gaskets. If the mounting nuts have been overtightened, this plate may have cracked. If so, fit a new plate, making sure that it is exactly the same thickness as the old one because this governs the distance the fuel pump lever travels.

If there is still a leak from the pump, the pump oil seal may have failed. The pump will then need overhauling or renewing.

Timing cover

A common source of oil leaks is the seal for the timing cover at the crankshaft-pulley end of the engine. Look at the nearby bodywork and engine parts for signs of oil having been flung out sideways by the crankshaft pulley. Look also at the underside of the engine beneath the seal, and on the sump pan, for signs of oil streaks.

If the oil seal is leaking, the only cure is to fit a replacement. Make sure the rotating parts with which the seal is in contact are smooth and free of burrs or raised metal – they may well have caused the old seal to split and leak in the first place.

Crankshaft seal

The oil seal at the back of the crankshaft is usually hidden by the flywheel and the clutch housing, so the only visible sign of a leak from here is a drip from the bottom of the clutch housing. If you are experiencing clutch judder or slip you have another clue, as this is often caused by oil spraying on to the clutch plates.

To replace this seal you have to remove either the engine or the gearbox, which is probably best left

Check the oil filter for leaks

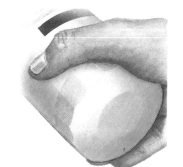

Make sure that a disposable oil filter is properly screwed into its mounting on the engine.

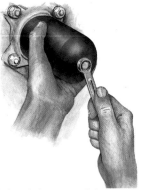

Check the tightness of the central bolt holding a replaceable-element filter to the engine.

to a garage because they have specialized equipment.

Oil sump pan

To check the sump pan thoroughly, raise the front of the car on ramps, apply the handbrake and chock the rear wheels so that you can safely get underneath the engine.

With the engine running, check for signs of oil leaks around the outside of the sump-pan mounting and also from the drain plug.

Look closely at the mounting flange around the crankshaft – sometimes the gasket here is in several parts, or there may be separate gaskets at the front and rear of the sump. These gaskets are liable to distort and leak, but make sure that the leak is not coming from the

oil seal at the front (pulley end) or rear of the crankshaft.

If the sump gasket is leaking, this may be because it has settled and contracted slightly. Cure the leak by tightening the sump mounting bolts or nuts, working gradually and evenly around the mounting flange. Do not overtighten them or you will distort the gasket. If this fails to cure the leak, you will have to fit a new gasket.

If the sump drain plug is the source of the leak, try tightening it. If that fails, the plug may not be fitted properly or its sealing washer may be leaking. Replace the washer and refit the plug correctly. If it still leaks, then the threads of the plug or the hole in the sump have probably been damaged. Consult a garage for advice.

Topping up with fresh oil

Once you've traced the source of the leak and cured it, you need to top up the engine with fresh oil or, if the existing oil is old, drain the system and refill with new oil.

Pour in the oil in small amounts, taking frequent readings with your dipstick. Once the level reaches the Full/Max mark, start the engine and allow it to idle for a few minutes so that the oil can be pumped round the engine.

Recheck the area round the source of the leak to make sure that it is cured. Then stop the engine, wait for a few minutes for the oil to drain back into the sump, and check the oil level again. Add a little more oil if necessary.

Replacing the engine's gaskets and oil seals

If your engine has developed a leak, the first step is to trace its source (see pages 43, 44, 45, 46). Having discovered the particular component responsible for the leak, try tightening up the nuts or bolts holding that component to the rest of the engine. If that fails, then the most likely cause of the leak is a worn gasket or oil seal, which you will have to replace.

Rocker cover gasket

To fit a new gasket to the rocker cover or camshaft cover, first examine the cover for any pipes or wires fixed or running close to it and remove them. For example, you may have to remove the spark plug leads or the breather pipe leading to the air cleaner before you can take off the cover.

The cover is fixed either by nuts or bolts through the top of the cover, or by screws around the side. Loosen them all first, then remove them along with any oil-sealing washers. If there is more than one washer on each bolt, note the order in which they come off.

Now carefully lift off the cover. If it sticks, give it a sideways tap with a soft-faced hammer or the palm of your hand. If it still won't move, lever it very gently upwards with a broad screwdriver blade, but take great care not to damage the cylinder head or rocker cover when you are doing this.

Scrape off gasket

Take off the old gasket from the cover flange or the cylinder head, whichever it is attached to. Note how it fits – some gaskets have tongues that fit into cut-outs in the flange; some are stuck to the flange with sealant; others just fit into the groove. The gasket may also be in more than one piece.

Cover the valve gear with a clean cloth to stop dirt getting in, then scrape off the old gasket with a piece of wood. You may have to use

advanced

Tools and materials

- ☐ Spanners and screwdrivers
- ☐ Soft-faced hammer
- ☐ Broad-bladed screwdriver
- ☐ New gaskets and oil seals as needed
- ☐ Clean rags
- ☐ Gasket sealant if necessary
- ☐ Old pencils
- ☐ Ramps
- ☐ Jack
- ☐ Blocks of wood
- ☐ Stiff wire brush
- ☐ Torque wrench
- ☐ Tyre lever
- ☐ Universal puller
- ☐ Wet-and-dry paper

Removing a rocker cover gasket

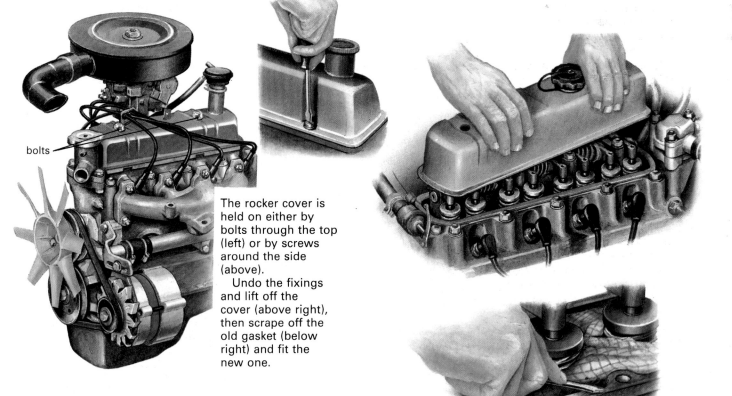

bolts

The rocker cover is held on either by bolts through the top (left) or by screws around the side (above).

Undo the fixings and lift off the cover (above right), then scrape off the old gasket (below right) and fit the new one.

a broad-bladed screwdriver for the last remains – take care not to scratch the cylinder head.

Carefully lift off the cloth and fit the new gasket to either the cover or the head, whichever the old one was fitted to. If the gasket has tongues, fit them into their cut-outs. If sealant was used on the old gasket, use it on both the new one and the cover; let it dry for a few minutes before fitting.

Refit the rocker or camshaft cover, aligning its fixing holes with those on the cylinder head. Check that the edge of the gasket aligns with the cover flange all the way round and is not distorted.

Tighten the nuts or bolts evenly to just nip the gasket. Reconnect any pipes and wires, start the engine and check that there are no longer any leaks.

Distributor seals

The distributor generally has an oil seal or gasket round its mounting flange where its drive passes into the crankcase or camshaft. You first have to take the distributor out of the car.

The distributor may have a rubber 'O' ring oil seal round its base or it may have a paper gasket under the plate of its securing clamp. In either case, discard the old seal or gasket, clean away all dirt and oil from the area and fit the new seal or gasket.

Refit the distributor, making sure that it goes back in exactly the same position as it came out.

Set the ignition timing statically to enable you to start the engine, then run the engine to make sure that there are no oil leaks. Finally, reset the ignition timing strobo-scopically.

Fuel pump gasket

Only mechanical fuel pumps are attached directly to the engine and therefore have gaskets; electrical pumps are always mounted away from the engine.

First disconnect the battery earth terminal to avoid any chance of a spark while the fuel pipes are disconnected. Unscrew the pipe connections and plug each with an old

Replacing a distributor seal or gasket

To do this you need to remove the distributor. First take off the cap and turn the engine over until the rotor arm is pointing to the plug contact of the timing cylinder and the timing marks on the pulley point to TDC.

Then mark the rotor arm position on the distributor body (**1**) and disconnect the LT lead. Loosen the securing clamp bolt at the base of the distributor and pull the distributor out (**2**).

There will be either a paper gasket under the securing clamp (**3**) or a rubber 'O' ring oil seal round the base of the distributor. Remove it and fit a new one.

1 Mark position of rotor arm on distributor body.

2 Loosen the clamp securing bolt.

3 Remove the paper gasket (as here) or 'O' ring oil seal.

Replacing a mechanical fuel pump gasket

As you are dealing with the fuel system, first disconnect the battery earth terminal as a safety measure.

Then undo the clips holding the fuel pipes to the pump (**1**) and plug each pipe with a pencil to stop the fuel pouring out (**2**).

Now undo the two nuts or bolts holding the pump to the engine (**3**) and pull off the pump. There may be a spacer gasket sandwiched between two thin gaskets (**4**), in which case make sure that the new spacer gasket is exactly the same thickness as the old one.

1 Unscrew clips holding fuel pipes to the pump.

2 Use a pencil to plug each pipe.

3 Unbolt the pump from the engine.

spacer

4 Sometimes there is a spacer gasket. Make sure the new one is the same size.

pencil. Remove the nuts or bolts holding the pump in place and pull the pump, with its gasket or gaskets, off the engine.

There may be a single gasket or a thick spacer gasket sandwiched between two thin paper gaskets. Check the spacer for cracks and replace it if you see any. In any case, replace the two thin gaskets. If buying a new spacer gasket, make sure it is exactly the same thickness as the old one – this thickness governs the fuel-pump lever stroke.

Remove all traces of gasket from the pump and the engine. Fit the new gasket or gaskets, reconnect the pump and tighten the fixings. Make sure the fuel pipe connections are clean, then unplug them and refit them to the pump. Reconnect the battery, start the engine and check again for leaks.

Drop the sump

If the source of the leak seems to be the sump gasket, you will probably be able to fit the new gasket without having to take the engine out of the car. But if you find that the suspension cross-member won't allow you to remove the sump completely from the engine, you have to jack the engine up, support it on its mountings, then disconnect the sump and drop it down far enough to fit the new gasket.

To do this, first raise the front of the car on ramps, apply the

handbrake and chock the rear wheels. Drain the oil from the sump, then clean around the sump area.

Put a block of wood at least 6in (150mm) thick between jack and sump to prevent any damage to the sump, then jack up the sump. Make sure you don't strain the cooling hoses or any other connections – if necessary, disconnect them.

Have a friend ready to steady the engine while you undo the mounting nuts or bolts, then raise the engine about 1½in (40mm) further. Insert wooden wedges between the engine and its mounting points. Once the engine is secure, remove the jack.

Remove sump gasket

Loosen all the sump nuts – on some cars you have to remove the clutch housing cover to get at the rear nuts. Remove all but a few nuts, then support the sump with one hand while you take out the remaining nuts with the other. Carefully lower the sump from the crankcase. You may need to turn the crankshaft over so that it protrudes less.

Scrape off all the traces of the old gasket, then clean out the inside of the sump with petrol and a stiff wire brush. Dry with a non-fluffy (lint-free) cloth.

Sump gaskets usually come in several pieces, often with separate curved seals that fit under the front and rear main-bearing housing of the crankshaft. Coat the sump

Preparing to drop sump

To get the extra space you need to drop the sump, jack up the sump and engine (above), using a wooden block under the sump to protect it.

Release the engine from its mountings, raise the jack a little higher, then insert wooden supports into the mountings (below) to support the engine while you release the sump.

Replacing a sump gasket

1 Use a socket spanner to loosen all the nuts or bolts holding the sump to the engine.

2 You may need to remove the clutch housing cover to get at the rear sump bolts.

3 There may be a curved gasket that fits round the crankshaft bearing cap. Replace it.

4 Remove the old gasket from around the sump and fit the new one. It may come in several pieces.

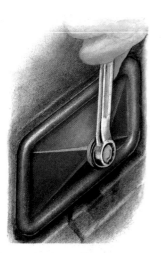

Side cover gaskets

Some engines have crankcase side covers, whose gaskets are a possible source of a leak. The cover may be held on by a central bolt (above) or by a series of screws around the side.

Undo the fixings and remove the cover (you may need to take off a manifold first). Scrape off the old gasket and fit the new one.

flange with sealant (and, if necessary, the grooves for the curved pieces) and fit the gasket.

Refit the sump, taking great care not to disturb the gasket. Tighten all the fixings in sequence to the correct torque (consult a manual or your dealer). Raise the engine with the jack just enough to allow you to remove the wedge supports, then lower the engine on to its mountings, do up the mountings loosely and lower the jack.

Replace the sump plug, fill the engine with oil, start it and check for leaks around the sump flange. If all seems well, stop the engine and tighten the mountings.

Front oil seal

On most cars you have to remove several parts before you can get at the oil seal at the front of the crankshaft. First slacken the generator pivot bolts, swing the generator away and slip off the drive belt. If necessary, remove the radiator to make room for removing the crankshaft pulley.

If the car has a manual gearbox, select first or reverse gear and put the handbrake on. For an automatic, disconnect the battery and remove the starter motor. Insert a tyre lever or a large screwdriver into

the starter aperture so that it jams into the teeth of the ring gear on the flywheel.

Unscrew the pulley bolt (it undoes in the opposite direction to the rotation of the engine). Slide off the pulley; if necessary, use a universal puller to remove it. A Woodruff key fits on the crankshaft and pulley to stop the pulley turning on the crankshaft. Remove the key and keep it somewhere safe.

You should now be able to see the outer end of the oil seal. If not, you need to remove the timing-belt cover or chain cover and possibly the water pump. Clean around the oil seal and check how it fits.

Lever the seal out with a screwdriver, taking care not to score the seal housing. Clean around the housing and set the new seal in place with its open (spring) side towards the engine. Put a wooden block or a large tube against the seal and tap it squarely into the housing until it is fully home.

Thoroughly clean the sleeve at the back of the pulley; rub down any rough areas with wet-and-dry paper. Smear clean engine oil on the pulley sleeve then refit the pulley and reposition the key. Tighten the pulley bolt to the correct torque, then refit all the components in the reverse order to removal.

Replacing a crankshaft front oil seal

Having gained access to the crankshaft pulley, jam the flywheel ring gear to stop the engine turning over, then undo the pulley bolt (1).

You may be able to remove the pulley by hand, but more likely you will need to use a universal puller to do this (2).

Use a pair of pliers to carefully remove the Woodruff key that holds the pulley shaft to the crankshaft (3).

Prise out the old oil seal with a screwdriver, taking care not to damage the housing (4), then tap in the new seal using a wooden block to protect it (5).

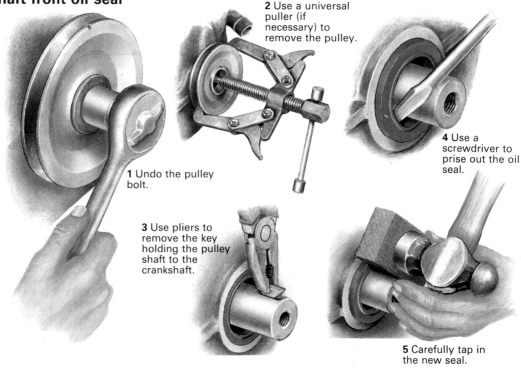

1 Undo the pulley bolt.

2 Use a universal puller (if necessary) to remove the pulley.

3 Use pliers to remove the key holding the pulley shaft to the crankshaft.

4 Use a screwdriver to prise out the oil seal.

5 Carefully tap in the new seal.

Introducing the brakes

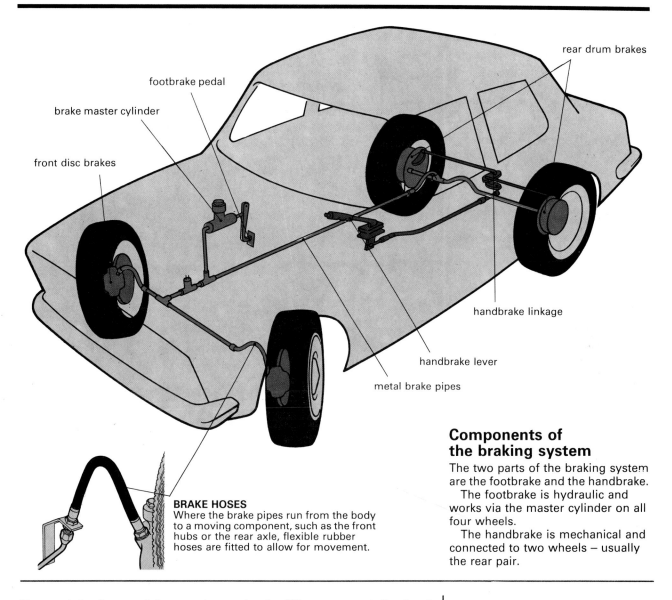

rear drum brakes

footbrake pedal

brake master cylinder

front disc brakes

handbrake linkage

handbrake lever

metal brake pipes

BRAKE HOSES
Where the brake pipes run from the body to a moving component, such as the front hubs or the rear axle, flexible rubber hoses are fitted to allow for movement.

Components of the braking system

The two parts of the braking system are the footbrake and the handbrake.

The footbrake is hydraulic and works via the master cylinder on all four wheels.

The handbrake is mechanical and connected to two wheels – usually the rear pair.

Your car's brakes work by creating friction between a fixed part of the car and a drum or disc turning with the road wheels. The friction between the two slows the wheels.

All cars have two separate braking systems – the footbrake and the handbrake. For safety reasons, if the footbrake fails you need to be able to use the handbrake to bring the car to a halt. So the footbrake and the handbrake are independent of each other and work in different ways.

Mechanical brakes

The handbrake is mechanically operated and works on just two wheels. When you put the handbrake on, it pulls on a series of cables and/or rods to operate the brakes. Usually the handbrake works on the rear wheels but on a few cars, such as the Citroen 2CV, it works on the front instead.

Hydraulic brakes

The footbrake is hydraulically operated and works on all four wheels. The brake pedal is attached to the **master cylinder** by a rod. From this cylinder a system of pipes runs out to the brake at each wheel. The pipes and the cylinder are filled with a special fluid called **brake fluid** which has a high boiling point

Disc or drum?

Cars can be fitted with either disc brakes or drum brakes. Older cars had drum brakes on all four wheels, while modern high-performance cars have discs on all four. Today, however, most cars compromise with disc brakes on the front wheels and drum on the rear.

Inside a drum brake

Shown below is a typical drum brake assembly, cut away to reveal the components inside. Some drum brakes have one cylinder (as here), others two. Nevertheless they work in much the same way.

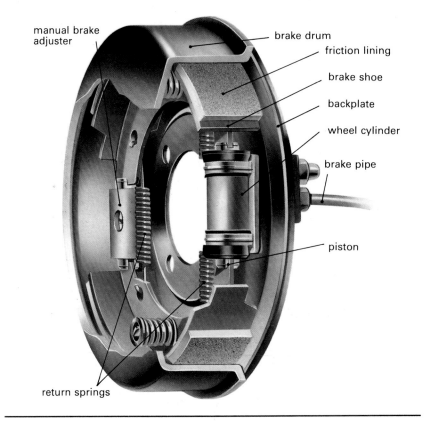

manual brake adjuster

brake drum

friction lining

brake shoe

backplate

wheel cylinder

brake pipe

piston

return springs

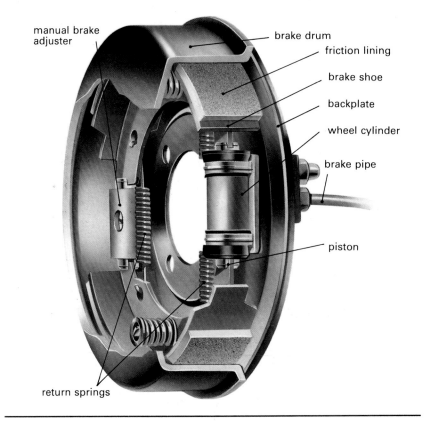

outboard

inboard

Outboard or inboard?

The brakes are usually mounted just inside the wheels (the outboard position) but some manufacturers fit them nearer the centre of the car at the inner ends of the drive shafts (the inboard position).

The advantage of inboard brakes is that they reduce the weight of the wheel hubs, making the car handle better. Their disadvantage is that they are more inaccessible, and therefore difficult to work on, and they are also vulnerable to oil leaks from the engine, gearbox or axle.

The Citroen 2CV and GS, and the Alfasuds have inboard brakes on the front wheels, and the Rover 2000 and 2200 have them on the back.

The brake servo

You need to exert much more force on the footbrake to operate a disc brake than you do a drum brake. So most modern cars are fitted with a brake servo to help with this greater effort.

When you put your foot on the brake the servo utilizes the vacuum created in the engine's inlet manifold to boost your foot pressure, which in turn increases the pressure on the brakes.

Drum brakes are rarely fitted with a servo. As well as being lighter to operate they also have a self-servoing effect. As the shoes touch the drum the drag of the turning drum pulls the shoes into even harder contact, making the brakes more powerful.

so the heat of braking does not cause it to boil.

The brake fluid is stored in a **reservoir** mounted on or close to the master cylinder. The reservoir holds enough fluid so that, if a leak occurs, you are unlikely to lose braking power immediately.

When you press the brake pedal a piston inside the master cylinder pushes fluid out of the cylinder and along the pipes to the brakes. Inside each brake the pressure of the fluid forces another piston in a cylinder to move, and this movement operates the brake, which is one of two types – drum or disc.

Drum brakes

A drum brake consists of a cast-iron drum attached to the wheel hub (and therefore turning with the wheel) and a metal plate called the **backplate** bolted to a fixed part of the axle so it does not move.

Inside the drum is a pair of almost semi-circular 'shoes' faced with a hard-wearing friction lining. One end of each shoe sits on the end of a piston inside a cylinder – the cylinder completes the circle formed by the two shoes. The other ends of the shoes are pivoted together.

The shoes and cylinder are mounted on the backplate – they are fixed and do not move with the wheels. When you put your foot on the brake, hydraulic fluid flows into the cylinder, forcing the pistons to move apart. These in turn force the shoes outwards and they press against the inner wall of the drum, causing the wheel to slow down.

When you take your foot off the brake a pair of springs inside the drum pulls the shoes back towards each other, releasing the pressure on the drum.

Disc brakes

A disc brake consists of a cast-iron disc attached to the hub and turning with the wheel. Straddling part of the disc is a **caliper** housing a pair

Disc brake assembly

Unlike the shoes of a drum brake, which are concealed, the pads of a disc brake are visible from the outside. The pistons and cylinders lie inside the caliper on the outer side of the pads.

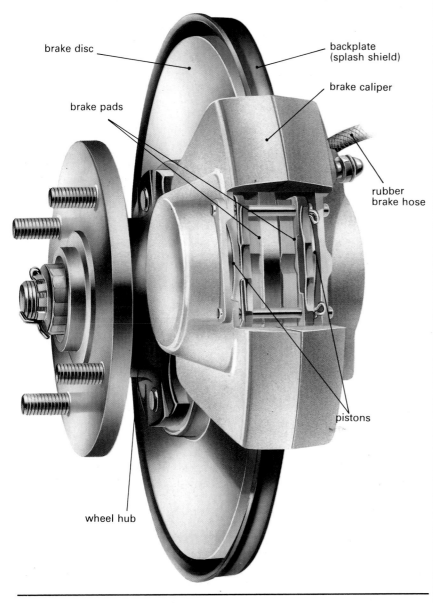

brake disc

brake pads

wheel hub

backplate (splash shield)

brake caliper

rubber brake hose

pistons

of friction pads (one on each side of the disc), and the cylinders, pistons and pipes that connect the pads to the hydraulic system.

When you put your foot on the brake, fluid passes into the cylinder and forces the pistons apart, squeezing the brake pads against the disc and slowing it down.

Calipers come in several designs and may contain one, two or four pistons. An opening in the caliper allows you to see the friction pads and so judge how worn they are. As the pads become worn down with use, the pistons slip forward to maintain a constant gap between the pads and the disc.

Pros and cons

Disc brakes are superior to drum for several reasons. One is that they are self-adjusting – the gap be-

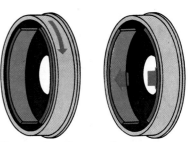

Drum brake action

Two curved shoes, each with special friction lining, are forced apart by a pair of pistons and press against the inside of the drum.

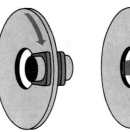
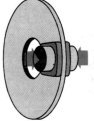

Disc brake action

A pair of pads, lined with friction material, are forced together by pistons and press against each side of the disc.

Friction material

Brake pads and brake shoes are both lined with special friction material. On pads a roughly square block of the material is bonded to a metal backing plate. Shoes have a much longer piece of the material bonded or riveted to the curved edge of the metal shoe.

On most cars the friction material contains asbetos for its excellent heat-resisting qualities. But, with the growing concern over the danger of asbestos in the air, some manufacturers are now producing asbestos-free friction materials.

⚠ Brake fade

When the brakes are used continuously over a distance (for example, when driving down a steep mountain road) they overheat. This alters the frictional properties of the brake shoes and linings, reducing the braking power and increasing the amount of effort you have to apply to the pedal.

The effect is known as brake fade and affects mainly drum brakes because they are more likely to overheat more easily than disc brakes.

The problem of brake fade is worse if the brake fluid is old as it may have absorbed moisture from the air. If so, overheating causes this water to boil, forming bubbles in the fluid and making the pedal spongy. You may even lose the brakes altogether.

When driving down hills you should always select a lower gear instead of relying on your brakes.

tween the pads and the disc stays constant. Drum brakes can be made self-adjusting, but they are often unreliable.

A more important reason lies in the design of drum brakes. Because the drum is enclosed the heat generated during braking is not easily dispersed. On a steep downward incline a great deal of heat can build up and lead to a loss of braking power – an effect known as brake fade (see sideline).

The shape of the drum prevents rain, ice and grit or other debris getting into the brake, but it also means that if you totally immerse the brakes in water, by driving through a ford, for example, they will flood. You need to pump the brake pedal a few times so that the heat dries them out and braking is restored.

Disc brakes largely avoid the problem of fade and flooding because their open design allows heat and water to be dispersed quickly.

Despite these advantages most cars still have disc brakes only on the front wheels. This is because, when you brake, the weight of the car is thrown on to the front wheels. The front brakes have to take most of the strain of braking and can easily overheat, so disc brakes are fitted.

Rear brakes are still usually drum. As well as being cheaper, their shoes need renewing less frequently because their wear is spread over a wider area of friction material, and they also do much less of the braking.

The handbrake

When you operate the handbrake it pulls on a series of cables or rods 'linked, in most cases, to drum brakes on the rear wheels. This forces the same pair of brake shoes as those used by the footbrake into contact with the drums, locking the wheel into position.

Another reason why most cars still have drum brakes on rear wheels is that is much easier to connect the handbrake to a drum than to a disc brake. Cars with rear wheel disc brakes usually have the hand-brake connected to a separate set of smaller brake pads.

The handbrake mechanism

The handbrake is engaged by pressing its release button and pulling up the lever. This movement tugs on a cable inside the handbrake, pulling the brake shoes or pads into operation mechanically – usually on the rear wheels.

On some cars the handbrake is connected to two cables, one for each brake.

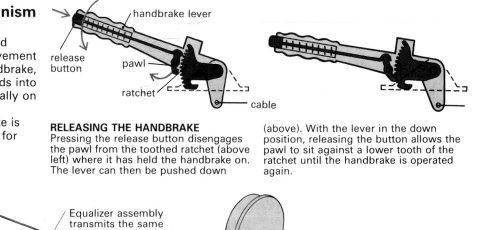

RELEASING THE HANDBRAKE
Pressing the release button disengages the pawl from the toothed ratchet (above left) where it has held the handbrake on. The lever can then be pushed down

(above). With the lever in the down position, releasing the button allows the pawl to sit against a lower tooth of the ratchet until the handbrake is operated again.

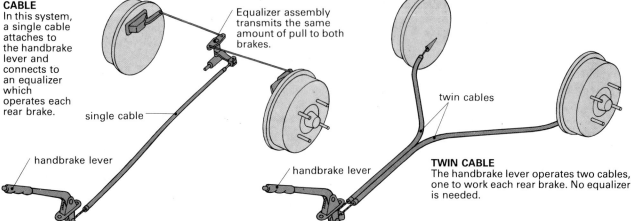

SINGLE CABLE
In this system, a single cable attaches to the handbrake lever and connects to an equalizer which operates each rear brake.

single cable

handbrake lever

Equalizer assembly transmits the same amount of pull to both brakes.

twin cables

handbrake lever

TWIN CABLE
The handbrake lever operates two cables, one to work each rear brake. No equalizer is needed.

Fitting new disc brake pads

The brake pads must be checked for wear at the service interval specified by the manufacturer – usually every 6000 miles (10,000km), but often every 12,000 miles (20,000km).

The minimum allowable thickness for the pads is usually $\frac{1}{16}$in (1.6mm), but this is the absolute limit. In practice it is safer to consider $\frac{1}{8}$in (3.2mm) as the minimum – the last area of pad can wear away in only a few hundred miles' motoring.

Always buy new pads of a reputable make. They come in sets of four – two for each wheel. Make sure you specify the exact model of your car, and whether it has servo-assisted brakes. Try to find out which make of brakes your car is fitted with.

Asbestos

Always be careful when working on the brakes, since the friction material used in the brake pads is usually asbestos-based – only a few cars are fitted with asbestos-free brakes.

Wear a face mask, or be very careful not to inhale any of the brake dust that may become dislodged. Wipe over the caliper and the pads with a damp cloth to remove loose dust.

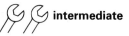 intermediate

Tools and materials

- [ ] Jack and axle stands
- [ ] Brake pads
- [ ] Pliers and screwdrivers
- [ ] Face mask
- [ ] Piston retracting tool or G-clamp
- [ ] Copper-based grease or special brake grease
- [ ] Rags
- [ ] Bleed tube and old jar
- [ ] Fresh brake fluid
- [ ] Coarse emery cloth

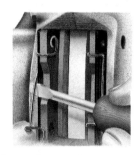
pads

Check the wear

On many cars, you can check the condition of the brake pads simply by looking through the wheel slots (as above).

But you may have to get under the car to inspect the pads, and on some cars you have to remove the wheels to do this.

Anti-rattle springs

You may find that your brake pads have anti-rattle springs fitted, like those shown above. They fit around the brake pad retaining pins and bear against the brake pads. They are easily prised free when removing the brake pads, but take care not to bend them out of shape, and note exactly how they fit.

The fixed caliper disc brake

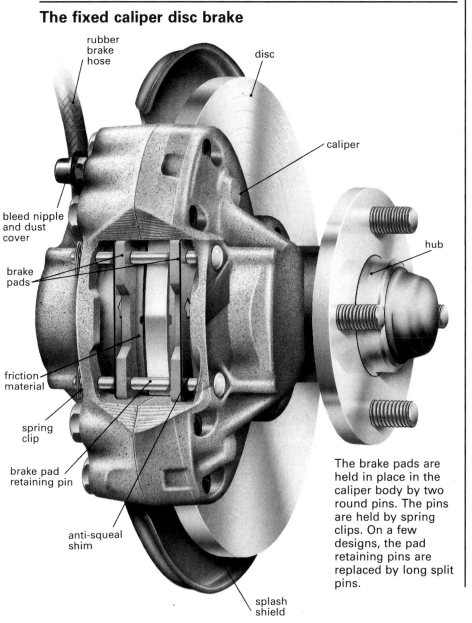

rubber brake hose

disc

caliper

bleed nipple and dust cover

hub

brake pads

friction material

spring clip

brake pad retaining pin

anti-squeal shim

splash shield

The brake pads are held in place in the caliper body by two round pins. The pins are held by spring clips. On a few designs, the pad retaining pins are replaced by long split pins.

Step-by-step guide to new pads

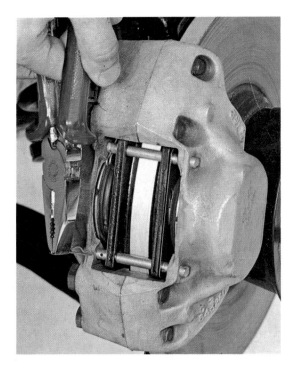

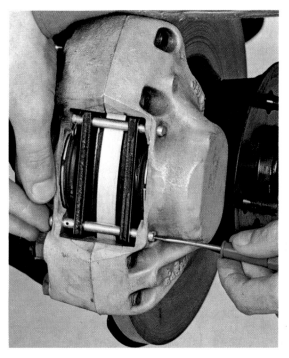

1 Jack up the car, support it on axle stands, and take off the wheels. Use pliers to remove the small R-shaped spring clip from the end of the retaining pin. If small split pins are used, straighten the bent ends and pull them out.

2 Try to push out the retaining pins with a thin screwdriver. If they have seized in place, use a little penetrating oil on them, then gently knock each retaining pin loose with a hammer and drift.

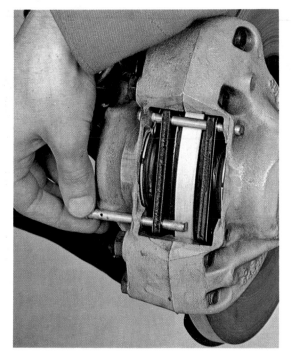

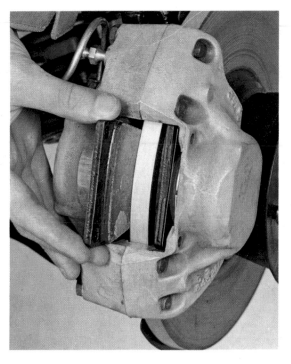

3 Once the pins are halfway out, you should be able to withdraw them by hand. If they snag on the pads or the anti-squeal shims, wiggle the pad, or the shim, into or out of the caliper until you can withdraw the pin.

4 The brake pads can now be pulled from the caliper. They are likely to be a very tight fit, so you may need to use pliers. Ensure you pull straight outwards otherwise the pad will jam. Don't forget to remove the anti-squeal shim.

5 Compare the old and new pads to make sure that they match exactly. If one of the old pads is more worn than the rest, or both pads on one side have worn more, the caliper is seized and needs freeing.

6 Clean off any rusty ridges from the edges of the disc (see overleaf). The pistons must be retracted into the caliper to allow for the thickness of the new pads. Lever them back with a special tool (as here) or other suitable lever.

7 Clean up the area where the pads fit using a damp rag. Take care not to inhale any dust. Smear brake grease on the rear of the pad and on the anti-squeal shim. Slip the pad home, then slide the shim between the pad and piston.

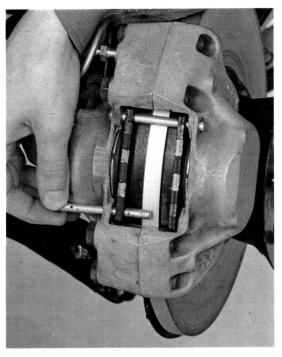

8 Clean up the retaining pins with wet-or-dry paper until shiny. Then push each one into the caliper so that it goes through the holes in the brake pads and shims. Refit the spring clips, then pump the brake pedal to take up the slack.

Cleaning the discs

When you remove the brake pads you will usually find that the brake disc has a ridge of rust running around the outer rim. If so, take the opportunity to remove it – if you don't, this rust will wear out the edge of the brake pad material and then gradually work its way across the disc, cutting down on the effective braking area.

If the ridge of rust is very slight, you can rub it off with emery cloth, while you rotate the disc by hand (below). Remove a larger ridge by running the disc round against a flat-bladed screwdriver braced in the caliper. Clean out all the debris with a wet rag.

Remove any rust ridge from the rim of the disc using coarse emery cloth or a screwdriver.

When fitting new pads, it is always a good idea to smear the metal backing plate with a proprietary brake grease (also known as anti-squeal grease) to prevent the brakes from squealing when you apply them (below). Do this even if your brakes are fitted with anti-squeal shims.

Take great care not to get any of the grease on to the friction material of the pad, otherwise the braking will be impaired.

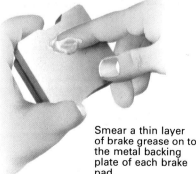

Smear a thin layer of brake grease on to the metal backing plate of each brake pad.

Levering back the pistons

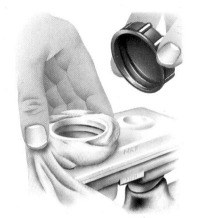

The new pads will be thicker than the old ones, so you need to push the pistons back to make room for them. This will force fluid back into the master cylinder, and if the level in the fluid reservoir is already high, there is a danger of fluid spilling out and running on to the paintwork and damaging it.

There are two ways you can prevent this happening. You can siphon fluid out of the fluid reservoir, or you can open the brake bleed nipple on the brake caliper and let the fluid escape along a bleed tube and into an old jam jar.

To remove fluid from the reservoir, wrap a rag around the filler neck to soak up spillages then use an old syringe. Don't try to suck fluid out with a tube – it is highly toxic. To bleed fluid out, first fit a ring spanner to the bleed nipple, then fit the bleed tube over the top. Immerse the end of the tube in a jar of brake fluid. Open the bleed nipple by about a half to a full turn, then use the piston retracting tool (see page 57), or a stout screwdriver, or a G-clamp if there is room, to retract the piston.

If you drained fluid from the reservoir, keep an eye on the level while you retract the pistons in case it rises too high – siphon off more fluid if you have to.

You may find that while retracting one piston, the other one tries to come out – simply slot the old brake pad in to stop it moving until you have retracted the other piston. Then fit the new pad in the retracted side, remove the old pad and retract the other piston. Once the pads are fitted, pump the brake pedal to take up the slack until the pedal is firm. Then top up the fluid reservoir to the 'max' level.

Before levering back the wrap some old rags around the neck of the brake fluid reservoir (left). This will soak up any excess fluid which might spill out and damage the paint.

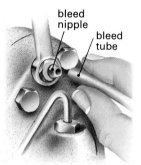

bleed nipple

bleed tube

If you are going to release the excess fluid through the brake bleed nipple, fit a bleed tube to the nipple, immerse the end of the tube in a jar of fluid, and open the bleed nipple with a spanner.

Lever the pistons back using a strong flat tool such as an engineer's screwdriver. Lever each piston back as far into the caliper as it will go.

If there is enough room you can use a G-clamp to retract the pistons. Take care to ensure that the piston goes back straight and does not jam.

Fitting new disc brake pads – 2

The previous four pages showed you how to service the most common design of caliper – the fixed caliper. But there are several other caliper designs found on a great many cars, including the Girling A sliding yoke caliper, the Girling XD48 fist caliper and the Girling/ATE Colette caliper. This chapter shows you how to change the pads on these three types of caliper.

Refer to pages 57, 58 before retracting the brake pistons; it contains valuable information on how to do the job. Also make sure you top up the brake fluid after changing the pads, and press the pedal a few times to take up the slack.

Bedding-in

Drive carefully for the first 50 miles (80km) or so, avoiding hard braking. This allows the pads to bed-in, and helps give them the maximum possible life.

 **intermediate**

Tools and materials

- ☐ New brake pads
- ☐ Spanners, screwdrivers and pliers
- ☐ 7mm Allen key, if necessary
- ☐ Releasing fluid (penetrating oil)
- ☐ Brake grease
- ☐ Hammer and drift
- ☐ New brake fluid
- ☐ Bleed tube and jam jar
- ☐ String

⚠ Don't touch the pedal

While the brake pads are out of the caliper, take great care not to touch the brake pedal. If you do, there is a risk of the pistons popping out of the caliper. You will then have a much larger repair job on your hands.

Sliding yoke caliper

The sliding yoke caliper has two pistons, both on the same (usually inner) side of the disc. When you brake, one piston presses the inner brake pad against the disc, while the other moves the sliding yoke to pull the outer pad into contact. The design shown here is the Girling A brake.

The brake pads are held in place either by a single U-shaped retaining pin locked home by a clip and a nut and bolt (see right) or by a pair of straight pins held by R-shaped spring clips.

Before taking out the retaining pins, remove the nut and bolt and clip or R-clips, and pull out the anti-rattle spring (**1**).

Spray the retaining pin or pins with releasing fluid, then pull them out. Use two pairs of pliers on a U-shaped pin to keep it straight or it will jam (**2**).

Next use the pliers to pull out the direct-acting pad – the one on the inside (**3**). On some cars there are wear sensor wires. If so, follow the wires back from the brake pad until you find their connection to the car's wiring and detach it.

To remove the indirect-acting pad, insert a stout screwdriver between the brake pad and the sliding yoke, and lever the yoke back until the pad is free. Watch the fluid level in the brake reservoir while doing this (see page 58).

Clean the caliper and the area where the pads sit. Also clean up the brake disc. Now lever back the sliding yoke far enough to fit the new indirect pad. Smear the back of the pad with brake grease and fit it.

Then lever back the piston for the new direct pad, and fit it, not

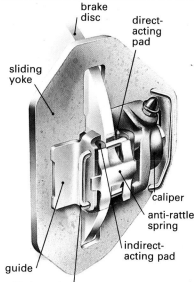

brake disc
sliding yoke
direct-acting pad
caliper
anti-rattle spring
indirect-acting pad
guide
U-shaped retaining pin

On this type of disc brake, the pads are held into the caliper either by a U-shaped pin (see left) or by a pair of straight pins.

1 For a U-shaped pin, remove its nut, bolt and clip, then lever off the anti-rattle spring (below left).

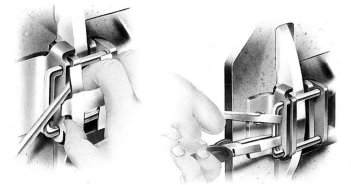

2 Pull out the pin (left), using two pairs of pliers to ensure it comes out straight.

3 Use pliers to pull out the direct pad (below), then lever back the yoke and remove the indirect pad.

forgetting the brake grease. Connect the wear sensor wires to the new pad. Fit the anti-rattle spring then the retaining pin or pins. Lock the pins in place with the clip or clips.

Pump the brake master cylinder by pressing the brake pedal a few times to take up any slack, then top up the reservoir to the correct level.

Colette caliper

Colette brakes, manufactured by Girling and ATE, have a single piston, with the caliper sliding on two guide pins. By removing the bolt holding one of the pins, the whole caliper can be swung out of the way to reveal the brake pads.

First detach the brake pad sensor wires at the connector. There is only one sensor on each side of the car, and it fits to the inner pad. Now find the bolt that fits to the guide pin – on most cars it is a normal hexagon head bolt, but on a few models it is a 7mm Allen bolt.

Use a spanner to hold the guide pin on the flats provided, then use another spanner or Allen key to undo the pin retaining bolt (**1**). Take care not to twist the rubber seals that fit on to the guide pin. With the bolt out, carefully swing the caliper away from the brake disc (**2**).

Prise the pads from the caliper (they may have a sticky backing) or lift them out of the mounting bracket. On some cars the anti-rattle springs are built into the pads, while others have separate springs (**2**).

Clean up the brake disc and retract the pistons as shown on the previous sheet. Fit the new pads, making sure that the one with the sensor wires fits to the inside. Swing the caliper back into position, being careful not to trap the sensor wires, then refit and tighten the guide pin retaining bolt. Reconnect the sensor wires and pump the brake pedal to take up the slack.

1 Hold the guide pin steady by gripping with a spanner on its flats, and undo the bolt with another spanner.

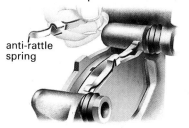

anti-rattle spring

2 Remove the bolt and swing the caliper body out to expose the brake pads.

Sliding (fist) caliper

The single-piston sliding caliper (also called a fist caliper), such as the Girling XD48, is found on many Ford cars. Similar designs by Freins Girling and Bendix are used on many French and Italian cars.

The piston sits on the inner side of the brake disc – when you brake, it presses one pad against the disc. At the same time, the caliper body slides sideways, pulling the other pad against the disc.

Start by wire-brushing all dirt and brake dust from the area around the retaining wedges. Now look for the retaining wedge clips. On Girling models there is a split pin that fits through a hole in the caliper body (see right). On other types the wedges have holes drilled in them into which fit R-clips.

Remove all the clips or split pins from both upper and lower wedges, then try to push out the wedge with a screwdriver (**1**). If it is stiff knock it out with a hammer and screwdriver. Note how it fits for reassembly. Knock out the lower wedge in the same way.

Push the caliper down slightly, then swing and pull it outwards to reveal the brake pads (**2**). Pull the caliper well clear – do not allow it to hang on the brake hose but tie it to a nearby component with string.

Now pull out each pad sideways (**3**). Anti-rattle springs are fitted to some pads. On Girling models they

are at the top end of each pad. On others you will find a clip running vertically along one edge.

Clean up the caliper where the pads fit, grease the back of each pad with brake grease, then fit the new pads and anti-rattle springs.

Retract the piston into the caliper (see pages 57, 58). Slide the caliper on to the pads, ensuring that it bears against the caliper springs. Holding the caliper in against the spring pressure, tap in the lower wedge. Then use a screwdriver to lever the caliper down and slide in the upper wedge.

Refit the split pins or the R-clips to hold the retaining wedges. Press on the brake pedal a few times to take up the slack.

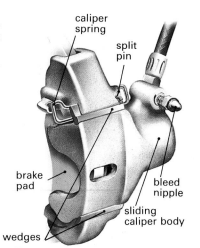

caliper spring

split pin

brake pad

bleed nipple

sliding caliper body

wedges

The fist caliper body slides along two wedges. Springs keep it firmly in place.

1 Pull out the split pins or R-shaped clips, then push out the wedges with a screwdriver.

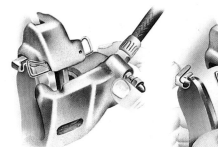

2 Push the caliper body down then out to clear the brake pads. Keep the caliper body supported.

3 Pull the pads out sideways.

Removing a disc brake caliper

Removing the brake calipers from your car is a fairly easy operation in most cases, though the best way to go about the job will depend on the reason you are removing them. If you are going to fit new seals, or otherwise service the caliper itself you will need to take it right off the car.

However, if you are removing the caliper to work on the suspension, steering, wheel bearings or brake disc, you often do not have to disconnect the complete caliper. Releasing the fixings will let you lift the caliper assembly away from the suspension.

Prepare the car

Start by jacking up the appropriate corner of the car and taking the wheel off. Removing a caliper often involves releasing tight bolts or drifting out wedges so make sure the car is firmly supported on axle stands. To give yourself more working space and easier access turn the steering to full lock.

Dirt and oil can cause serious damage to the caliper bore and seals so brush the outside of the caliper clean before you start dismantling. Alternatively wash the caliper down with hot soapy water.

In most cases removing the caliper means you first have to take off the brake pads (see pages 55 to 60).

If you intend to reuse the old pads, mark them to show which side of the disc they came from. This will ensure that they match up properly when replaced and so will not need much bedding in.

The movement of the pistons as

⚙⚙ **intermediate**

Tools and materials

☐ Jack and axle stands
☐ Spanners
☐ Pliers
☐ Screwdriver

As necessary:
☐ Wire brush
☐ Allen key
☐ Drift and hammer
☐ Brake fluid
☐ Copper-based grease
☐ Lock tabs
☐ Thread locking compound

Four types of caliper

Before you take off a caliper you need to know which type your car is fitted with, because the procedure for removal is different in each case.

Compare your car's calipers with the four types shown here. These are the most common types and are the ones covered in these sheets.

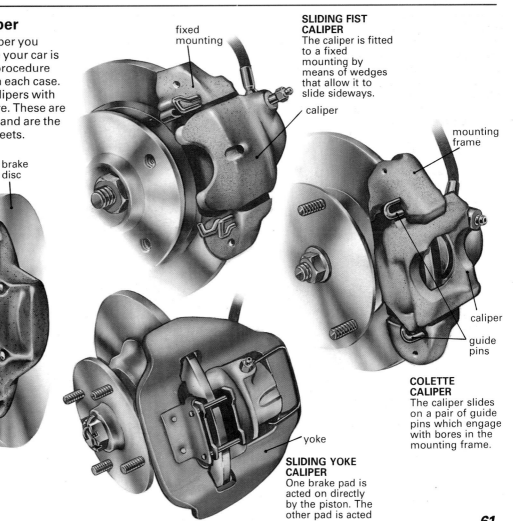

FIXED CALIPER
The caliper body is bolted to a non-moving part of the stub axle.

brake hose
brake disc
brake pads
piston
caliper

fixed mounting

SLIDING FIST CALIPER
The caliper is fitted to a fixed mounting by means of wedges that allow it to slide sideways.

caliper

mounting frame

caliper

guide pins

COLETTE CALIPER
The caliper slides on a pair of guide pins which engage with bores in the mounting frame.

yoke

SLIDING YOKE CALIPER
One brake pad is acted on directly by the piston. The other pad is acted on indirectly via a yoke.

⚠️ Keep it clean

When you disconnect the brake hose, it is essential to keep the sealing surfaces as clean as possible since even a small amount of dirt or grit can prevent the formation of a good seal.

Protect the ends of disconnected hoses or brake pipes by putting them into a plastic bag and taping it in place.

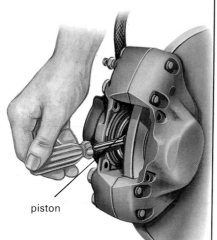

piston

Pumping out pistons

If you are going to overhaul the brake caliper by fitting new rubber seals, you will need to remove the piston or pistons from the caliper.

This is made much easier if you partially pump the piston out of its bore before you disconnect the brake pipe from the caliper. With the brake pads removed, ask a friend to gently press on the brake pedal so that the pistons move out. Use a screwdriver to prevent them from coming fully out (above).

When you come to overhaul the caliper, you should be able to pull out the piston with pliers.

you remove the caliper will force brake fluid back into the reservoir. To prevent an overflow remove some of the fluid with a syringe – though this may not be necessary if the level is already low.

Undo hoses

The next step is to disconnect the brake hose leading into the caliper. With many designs the flexible hose screws into a tapped bore in the caliper. The seal between hose and caliper may be made in two ways; by a soft metal sealing washer compressed between a flange on the hose thread and the caliper body; or by the end of the hose thread mating on a seating at the bottom of the bore in the caliper.

In both cases, first clamp the hose to minimize the loss of brake fluid, then disconnect the hose by unscrewing it from the caliper; this can often be done by rotating the caliper after removal.

Another design has a banjo coupling on the end of the hose with a hollow bolt passing through the banjo bore and into a tapped hole in the caliper. Here the seal is formed

by washers fitted between the mating surfaces while the hose is disconnected, after first clamping it, by undoing the bolt.

In some cases the hose does not connect directly to the caliper. Instead there is an intermediate length of metal brake pipe running from a hose mounting on the suspension to the caliper. In this case you can clamp the hose, leave it in place and just undo the pipe fitting at the caliper.

You are now ready to remove the caliper. How you do this depends on the type of caliper you have. The four most popular types are covered on the following two pages.

Finishing off

With the caliper back in place, refit the hose, using new sealing washers if fitted. Bleed the brakes (only if you had to disconnect the caliper completely), then refit the wheel and lower the car to the ground. If you didn't have to disconnect the hose, you should still pump the brake pedal a few times to take up any free piston movement.

Finally, take the car for a run and try the brakes at low speed.

Preparatory work

Having first sprayed around the caliper with penetrating fluid, clamp the hose leading to the caliper (**1**). Then unscrew the hose from the caliper (**2**).

Alternatively there may be a rigid pipe leading into the caliper. If so, unscrew it (**3**).

1 Use a brake hose clamp to close off the hose.

2 Loosen the hose from the caliper – if possible unscrew the hose completely.

3 If there is a rigid pipe rather than a hose leading into the caliper, clamp the hose it attaches to then unscrew the union to release the pipe.

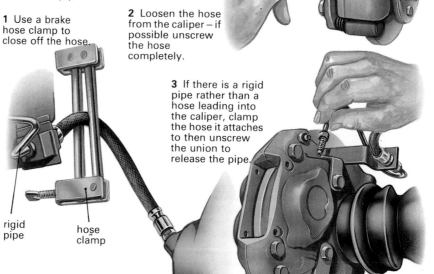

rigid pipe

hose clamp

Fixed calipers

The most straightforward type of caliper is the fixed caliper. This has two sets of pistons and cylinders, one on each side of the wheel, with the cylinders being connected by bores within the caliper.

The brake pads on this type of caliper fit into gaps between the pistons and the disc, and are held in place by pins.

To remove the pads withdraw the pin locking clips or straighten the end of the split pins, and pull the pins out of the calipers. Lift out any anti-rattle springs and use a pair of pliers to pull the pads up out of the caliper. Slacken the hose or pipe connection.

The caliper is directly mounted on to the fixed part of the stub axle assembly, generally with bolts fixed in threaded holes.

Knock back the locking tabs (**1**) and undo the bolts (**2**). Lift the caliper away, unscrewing it from the hose or pipe.

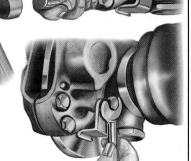

1 Bend back any locking tabs holding the caliper mounting bolts secure.

2 Undo the caliper mounting bolts and withdraw them.

Colette calipers

Another arrangement, sometimes known as the Colette caliper, is similar to the fist caliper but slides on a pair of guide pins which engage with bores in the mounting frame. The pins are located at the top and bottom of the caliper and are enclosed by protective dust shields.

First undo the brake hose by a fraction of a turn. Push the cylinder housing towards the brake disc to push the piston back into the cylinder and give a little clearance between pads and disc.

Use a spanner on the guide pin flats (on the disc side of the caliper) to stop the pin turning while you undo the lower mounting bolt (**1**).

Pivot the caliper upwards around the top guide pin and withdraw the pads. Swing the caliper down and use a spanner to hold the top guide pin while you remove the upper mounting bolt.

Then lift the caliper free (**2**) and unscrew it from the brake hose. If required remove the brake carrier from the stub axle assembly by undoing the mounting bolts.

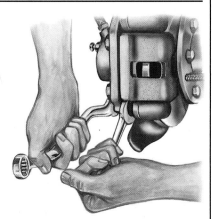

1 Hold the guide pin firm with one spanner while you undo the lower mounting bolt with another spanner.

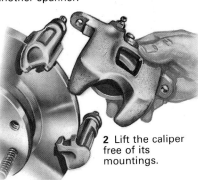

2 Lift the caliper free of its mountings.

☆ Mounting bolts

Generally the main caliper mounting bolts will be prevented from shaking loose by locking tabs or washers or, where through bolts are used, self-locking nuts.

But where there is no obvious locking device it is possible that a thread-locking compound has been used during assembly – inspect the thread to see if there are any traces of a plastic-like deposit.

You should use new lock tabs or washers when refitting the caliper, and tighten it to the specified torque (for most caliper mounting bolts this is of the order of 40 to 60lb ft, but check in a service manual or ask your dealer).

Where there is no obvious locking device, clean the thread and apply a few drops of thread-locking compound (above). Even if the assembly did not rely on thread locking it will not do any harm.

Sliding fist calipers

This type of caliper has a single hydraulic cylinder in a fist-shaped housing that fits over the brake disc with the bulk of the caliper to the inside of the disc.

The caliper assembly is mounted on a fixed mounting by means of wedges that allow it to slide sideways under the action of the piston so as to grip the disc between the brake pads.

Loosen the hose connection. Remove the locking clips in the ends of the wedges and push the wedges out from the gap between caliper and mounting (**1**). If there is any corrosion the wedges may be jammed in place, so use a hammer and drift to tap them free.

Push the caliper downwards into the space taken up by the lower wedge and pull the top edge out from the lip of the mounting. Lift the caliper up to free it from the bottom of the mounting and unscrew it from the brake hose (**2**).

The brake pads fit into shaped openings in the side of the mounting and can be pulled free along with the anti-rattle springs. The mounting itself is bolted to the suspension assembly and can be removed by undoing any locking tabs and unscrewing the bolts (**3**).

Before refitting the caliper, wire-brush the wedges and the mating faces on the caliper and mounting to remove any corrosion or built-up dirt and apply a thin coating of copper-

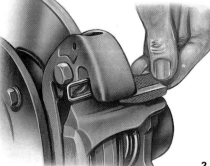

1 Knock out the wedges with a hammer and drift.

2 Unscrew the caliper from the brake hose.

3 Unbolt the caliper mounting from the stub axle.

4 Remove the caliper securing bolts with an Allen key.

based grease to the sliding faces.

Fit the brake pads and springs. Attach the brake hose and locate the lower end of the caliper in the mounting. Push the caliper down against the locating springs and swing it in to the disc to engage the upper mounting lip. Fit the lower wedge and use a screwdriver to lever the caliper into place so you can fit the second wedge. Tighten the brake hose.

A variation of this design does not have wedges. Instead the caliper is

carried on socket-head mounting bolts with bushes to allow sideways movement.

To remove this type the bolts are unscrewed using an Allen key (**4**) and the caliper lifted free. Depending on the design one or more of the pads may come away with the caliper, or they may be retained in the separate mounting assembly. If necessary remove this assembly by undoing the mounting bolts. Reverse the sequence to refit.

Sliding yoke calipers

Another design of single cylinder caliper has a fixed cylinder (inboard of the disc) with two opposed piston assemblies. One piston acts directly to force a brake pad against the brake disc. The other acts on a flat sliding yoke that sits over the disc and transfers the thrust to a second pad.

Remove the locking pins and the pad retaining pins and withdraw the brake pads and anti-rattle springs. In some designs the retaining pins are an interference fit and have to be drifted out with a punch.

Loosen the brake pipe coupling (**1**). Undo the bolts holding the cylinder assembly to the axle mounting (**2**), pull the caliper clear and unscrew it clear from the hose.

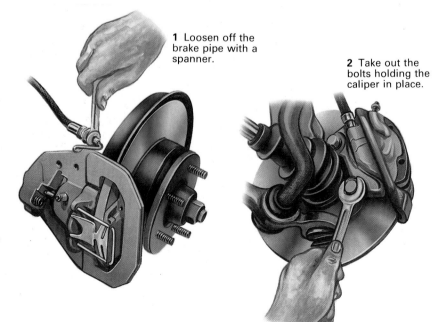

1 Loosen off the brake pipe with a spanner.

2 Take out the bolts holding the caliper in place.

Inspecting the drum brakes

You need to check drum brake linings for wear every six months, 6000 miles (10,000km) or as recommended in your car handbook. On some modern cars there is a plugged inspection hole in the backplate that you can look through to inspect the shoes. You may have to raise the car and support it on axle stands before you do this. On other cars you need to remove the drums to check the shoes' condition.

Raise the car

Most cars have drum brakes on the rear wheels only, if at all. Follow the usual procedure for removing a wheel, and chock the front wheels firmly at the front and back of each wheel. If you are examining front drum brakes, apply the handbrake to hold the car, and also chock the rear wheels.

Make sure you support the car on axle stands, not on a jack or bricks, especially if you have to get under the car (to look through an inspection hole for example).

If there is an inspection hole, unplug it then use a torch to inspect the lining. Try to judge how worn they are – if this is difficult, take off the drum and do the job as described for those cars without inspection holes. If the shoes are below the specified limit, you must buy new ones and fit them as described on pages 73, 74, 75, 76.

Removing the drums

If the brakes have manual adjusters, slacken them right off before you remove the drums to make the job easier (see pages 69, 70, 71, 72). With self-adjusting brakes, slackening is usually neither necessary nor easy.

There are two different designs of brake drum; one in which the drum and wheel hub are separate, and one in which they are integral. The removal procedure varies

Drum brake assembly, showing main parts

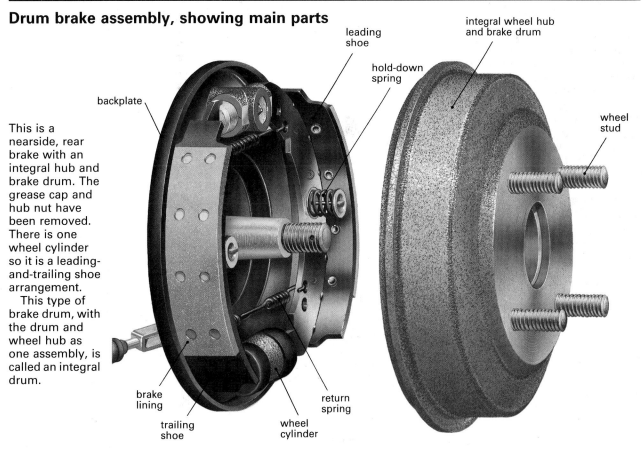

This is a nearside, rear brake with an integral hub and brake drum. The grease cap and hub nut have been removed. There is one wheel cylinder so it is a leading-and-trailing shoe arrangement.

This type of brake drum, with the drum and wheel hub as one assembly, is called an integral drum.

backplate

leading shoe

hold-down spring

integral wheel hub and brake drum

wheel stud

brake lining

trailing shoe

wheel cylinder

return spring

depending on which type you have – look in your car handbook.

Separate drum

The drum may be held to the hub by one or two screws or by bolts. Remove them – the screws are likely to be very tight so make sure that you have a large, well-fitting screwdriver. If the screws get chewed up, buy replacements. Alternatively the drum may be held on by a spring clip on one wheel stud, or there maybe no fixing at all.

Paint a mark on one wheel stud and against the hole through which it fits so that you can refit the drum in the same position. If the wheel has been balanced on the car, the balance of the brake drum will have been taken into account, so it's important to get the drum back in the same position.

Pull the drum straight off if you can. If it sticks, tap all round the edge of the drum – not the lip – with a soft-faced hammer. Do not try to lever the lip away from the back-plate – you may damage it.

If tapping fails to move the drum, put penetrating oil on the studs and the joint between the drum and the hub and leave it for a while. Alternatively, pour several kettles of boiling water over the drum to make it expand. Place a bucket beneath to catch scalding water.

Integral drum

Removing an integral drum is more complicated than removing a separate one because you are removing the hub as well.

First prise off the central grease cap with a screwdriver. Lever evenly round the edge – if it becomes crooked it will stick. If levering fails, tap gently round the edge with a hammer and chisel.

If the cap has no lip to give you leverage, drill a hole in it, insert a self-tapping screw and pull it with a claw hammer. Plug the hole before refitting the cap, or buy a new one as they are quite cheap. If all else fails, break off the cap with a hammer and chisel and fit a new one.

Under the cap there may be a castellated nut (sometimes called a

Removing a separate drum

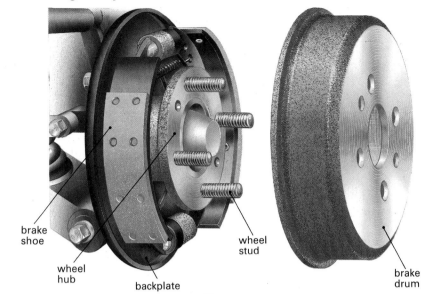

brake shoe

wheel hub

backplate

wheel stud

brake drum

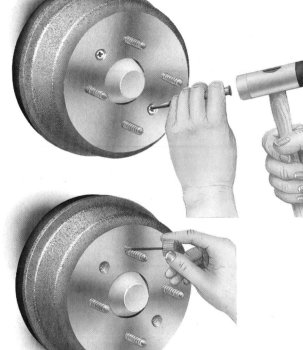

1 If the bolts or screws securing the drum are stubborn, tap them with a centre punch, offset from the slot, in the unscrewing direction.
Once the stubborn screw is loosened, finish unscrewing with a screwdriver.

2 Mark one wheel stud and hole with paint or nail varnish so that you can be certain to refit the drum in the same position.

3 If the drum sticks, tap around the edge with a soft-faced hammer. Take care not to hit the lip of the drum or the backplate. If you do, you may damage them and make reassembly difficult.

castle nut), or a castellated cap over a plain nut held by a split pin. Straighten the legs of the split pin and pull it out, after tapping it with a hammer if necessary. Always use a new split pin when reassembling. Remove the cap, if there is one.

Examine the nut carefully to see if it has a left-hand thread. The nuts on the nearside wheels usually have a left-hand thread to avoid the danger of the wheel's rotation spinning the nut loose.

Remove the nut. It is tightened to a precise torque, which varies greatly from car to car, so before refitting check the figure with your local dealer or car handbook.

If the nut is very tight, try to unscrew it with a socket wrench, using a piece of pipe over the handle to give extra leverage.

With the nut removed you may be able to pull off the drum and hub by hand. Spread a clean rag on the ground before you do this – some-times a bearing falls free as the hub comes off and you don't want to lose it or get it dirty.

If the assembly is stiff, try refitting the wheel and pulling that. Do not lever the lip of the drum or you may damage it. If it fails to come free after a reasonable amount of effort, you will need a universal hub puller – a special tool that you can buy or hire.

Measure the wear

With the drum off, you can see the brake shoes. The linings may be riveted or bonded (glued) on to the metal of the shoes. The simplest way to measure wear on shoes with riveted linings is to use a tyre tread depth gauge with the prong in the rivet hole. You should renew the shoes when the lining has worn down to $\frac{1}{16}$in (1.5mm) *above* the rivet heads.

If you have shoes with bonded

⚠ Asbestos

Be very careful not to breathe in dust when handling brakes. Asbestos, which is poisonous, is used in brake linings and is present in the dust. If possible, use a vacuum cleaner to remove the dust. Dispose of the bag carefully afterwards.

Removing an integral drum

First, prise off the central cap with a screwdriver, working evenly round its lip (**1**).

Then, pull out the split pin (**2**). Examine the exposed thread on the shaft to see if it is right- or left-hand thread. Undo the nut accordingly.

Finally, pull off the drum, by hand if possible (**3**). It should come away complete with bearings. Spread a clean rag on the ground to catch any that might fall.

1 Prise off the central cap.

2 Remove the split pin.

3 Pull off the drum by hand, if you can.

Check your tyres

Before renewing drum brakes, inspect the tyres. A worn tyre opposite a fairly new one will give unbalanced braking; so will two tyres inflated at different pressures and running on the same axle.

☆ Leaf springs

If your car has leaf spring suspension at the rear, check that the U-bolts securing the rear axle to the leaf springs are tight.

A loose-fitting U-bolt will let the axle roll and the brakes will seem to 'grab' on and off.

linings you can measure them with a ruler. You should renew them when the lining has worn down to ⅛in (3mm) thick, even if a minimum thickness of ¹⁄₁₆in (1.5mm) is quoted in your car handbook. The difference between ⅛in (3mm) and ¹⁄₁₆in (1.5mm) can disappear before you next service the brakes.

It is possible to have new linings riveted to old shoes. This is a specialist job, however – do not try to tackle it yourself. It is easier simply to buy new brake shoes from an accessory shop – you may even get money for the old shoes if they are sold on an exchange basis.

Always renew brake shoes on both wheels on an axle, even if one is more worn than the other. Also renew the shoes on both wheels if one lining has been fouled by oil or brake fluid.

Be careful when buying new brake shoes. Buy ones that have a well-known maker's name correctly spelt on the box and the part itself. Dangerous fakes are common and they often have names only slightly altered from a well-known make. Be suspicious of cheap parts. Changing the shoes is covered on pages 73, 74, 75, 76.

Refit the drum

Refitting is the reverse procedure of dismantling. Before you refit the drum, clean any brake dust from inside it and from the linings with a small brush. Be careful not to breathe any in. Remember that it contains poisonous asbestos.

If you are refitting an integral drum, do up the hub nut to the correct tightness using a torque wrench. Always fit a new split pin and refit the grease cap. Check in your handbook or ask your dealer for the correct figure.

Checking brake shoes for size and wear

Compare the new shoes with the old ones for correct size and type before you start dismantling (right). Measure the wear if you are uncertain whether you need new ones.

For riveted linings, use a tyre tread depth gauge to see if the linings have worn down to ¹⁄₁₆in (1.5mm) above the rivet heads (below). If so, they need replacing.

For bonded linings, measure with a ruler from the face of the shoe to the top of the lining (below right). Replace shoes that have worn down to ⅛in (3mm) thickness.

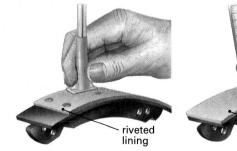

riveted lining

bonded lining

Adjusting drum brakes

snail cam

wheel cylinder

Snail cam adjuster

An adjuster peg passing through the backplate turns a snail cam against a peg on the brake shoe, forcing the shoes apart.

Most cars have disc brakes on the front wheels and drum brakes at the rear. With use, the pads (on disc brakes) and shoes (on drum brakes) wear down. This is not a problem with disc brakes – at least, not until they wear away completely – because the pads automatically adjust themselves for wear, keeping a constant gap between themselves and the disc.

Some designs of drum brake are also self-adjusting, especially on newer cars, but on older models you generally have to adjust them yourself.

The brake should be adjusted so that the shoe is almost touching the inside of the drum. Slight pressure on the brake pedal should make the shoe press against its drum instantly.

When to adjust

Most manufacturers recommend that you check your drum brakes every six months or 6000 miles (10,000km), whichever comes

 **intermediate**

Tools and materials

□ Screwdriver, spanner, or brake adjusting spanner for your car's brakes
□ Jack
□ Axle stands
□ Penetrating oil

Brake adjusters

Shown here are the three most common types of brake adjuster. They are all accessible mainly from the back of the brake drum. The fourth type – the screw-headed adjuster – is found mainly on older cars and is accessible from the front of the brake drum.

Wedge adjuster

Turning a square (sometimes hexagonal) peg clockwise drives a wedge or cone between two pistons and forces the shoes apart.

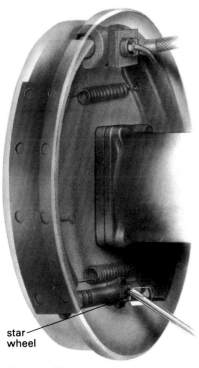

star wheel

Star adjuster

A star-wheel adjuster turns a threaded rod, which pushes the brake shoes apart.

securing stud

square-headed adjuster

brake backplate

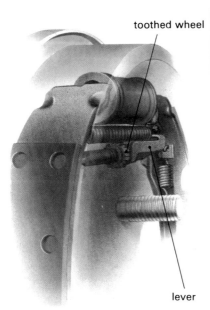

toothed wheel

lever

Automatic adjusters

Each time you brake, a lever in the drum brake turns a ratchet wheel and adjusts the brake shoes automatically.

sooner. You should also check the adjustment if you have to press the brake pedal down a long way before the brakes take effect, or if the car veers to one side during braking.

Most cars have a single adjuster but, where the drum brakes are on the front wheels, you will often find that two adjusters are fitted. Check in your handbook to find out how many there are on your car, their exact location and which type they are. There are four types of adjuster – wedge, snail cam, screw-headed and star wheel.

Wedge/snail cam

The wedge adjuster usually has a short square-shaped end sticking out of the brake backplate, but sometimes the head of the adjuster is hexagonal (bolt-shaped). The snail cam adjuster has a similar square or hexagonal head sticking

out of the backplate.

With both types, the end of the adjuster is often partly recessed or obscured, making it difficult to adjust, so always use the correct special brake adjusting spanner. Don't try to use an open-ended or ring spanner on square-headed adjusters.

Screw/star

Some models do not have the adjuster on the backplate. On a screw-headed adjuster there is a hole in the front of the brake drum through which you can insert a screwdriver to adjust the brakes.

Another type of adjuster is the star wheel or toothed wheel adjuster. This is accessible either through a hole in the front of the brake drum or through a hole in the brake backplate. The hole is usually blanked off by a bung to prevent dirt getting in.

Prepare to adjust

You may have to take the wheel off to get at the adjuster. To do this, first prise off the hub cap (taking care not to damage it by letting it fall on the road). Then with the car still on the ground, slacken the wheel nuts.

Jack up the appropriate side or end of the car, and support it securely on axle stands. Remember to chock the wheels that are still on the ground. Remove the wheel if necessary and place it under the car. Take care not to lose the wheel nuts. Release the handbrake if it operates on the drum you are working on. (Usually it operates on the rear wheels.)

The adjusters are exposed to weather and dirt, and are prone to seizing up. If you try to move them in a seized condition, you risk damaging or breaking off the adjuster. Lubricate each adjuster thoroughly with penetrating oil about two or three hours before you intend to start the job, and again just before you turn them. Take care not to apply too much oil in those cases where the adjuster is inside the brake drum.

Now go on to adjust whichever type of adjuster you have by referring to the next sheet.

1 Lever off the hub cap with a strong flat-bladed screwdriver.

2 While the wheel is still on the ground, slacken all the nuts with a wheel brace.

3 Place chocks under the wheel not being jacked up, then jack up the car.

4 Support the car on axle stands, then undo the nuts and remove the wheel.

Turning a screw-headed adjuster

This is the type of adjuster you can work on from the front of the wheel. Take off the hub cap and you will probably see a rubber bung in the wheel or brake drum. Prise it out with a slim screwdriver. Now insert your screwdriver into the hole (see right).

If there is no hole in the wheel you will have to remove the wheel to get at the adjuster. Turn the screw in the direction given in your handbook to move the shoes out to press against the brake drum. Then slacken it off just enough for the shoes to move back from the brake drum.

Check that the road wheel turns freely without any dragging from the brakes. If there is any drag, press the brake pedal down, then adjust again. Recheck that the wheel now turns easily.

⚠ **Brake spanners**

Always use a proper brake spanner when turning square-headed brake adjusters. These are available in both imperial and metric sizes to suit most cars. A flat spanner is adequate for most brakes, but if the adjuster is awkward to get at, buy a spanner with universally jointed swivel heads.

Adjusting wedge types

Wedge adjusters have a square-ended rod protruding from the brake backplate. Inside the drum, the other end of the rod is tapered to a cone or wedge shape (hence the name wedge adjuster). As the rod is screwed in or out, the taper moves between the ends of the brake shoes, forcing the shoes further apart or allowing them to close up.

Make the adjustment with a proper brake spanner, not an open-ended spanner. You may find that the adjuster is in such an awkward position that an ordinary flat brake spanner won't fit. If so, you need to use one of the swivel-headed span-ners (see right). This is slim enough to fit into even the most recessed space, and its universal joint allows you to clear obstructions.

Check in your handbook to see which way you should turn the adjuster – it may be clockwise or anti-clockwise. Fit the spanner over the end of the shaft, then turn the adjuster while you rotate the road wheel (or drum if the wheel is off) with your hand. When the wheel locks, back off the adjuster one click at a time until the wheel turns freely and you can hear the shoes just rubbing on the inside of the brake drum.

Adjusting a star wheel

Prise out the plug from the access hole and use a large flat-bladed screwdriver to turn the adjuster. Move it around by several teeth to make the brake shoes jam up against the brake drum. If the brakes do not lock up, you are turning the wrong way.

With the wheel locked on, use the screwdriver to turn the adjuster back by one or two clicks until the wheel spins freely.

Remove the plug in the backplate to gain access to the adjuster.

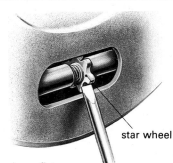

star wheel

Use a large flat-bladed screwdriver to turn the star wheel.

⚠ Get the balance right

When you adjust the drum brakes you should slacken off the adjuster until the wheel turns freely (as above).

Make sure that you adjust both brakes on the same axle by the same amount. If you don't, one brake will work before the other, making the car slew to one side during braking.

After adjusting the brakes, drive to a quiet stretch of road and check that the car pulls up straight under both gentle and hard braking. If it doesn't, try re-adjusting the brakes. If the problem persists the brakes need further checking – the brake cylinder may be leaky or partly seized up, or the brake shoes may be old or soaked with brake fluid.

Adjusting a snail cam

Press hard on the footbrake several times to centralize the brake shoes inside the brake drum. Check in your handbook to see which way you have to turn the adjuster – usually it is clockwise as viewed from the adjuster side.

Only use the correct spanner on the adjuster. Turn the adjuster until you feel a resistance, then try to turn the wheel. It should be locked.

Turn the adjuster back one click setting at a time until you can turn the wheel freely. A slight rubbing sound every now and again as the shoes touch a high spot in the drum is allowable.

There will be a certain amount of drag on the driven wheels caused by the transmission. Do not confuse this with brake drag. If you are unsure, check the wheel on the other side to compare.

If two adjusters are fitted, such as on the front brakes of Minis or Hillman Imps, then adjust one at a time until the brake locks, then back off until it frees. When you have finished, press the brake pedal to make sure the shoes are centralized to give even braking.

Using a proper brake spanner, turn the adjuster in the right direction (usually clockwise as you face it) until you feel resistance. The road wheel should now be locked.

Turn the adjuster back a click at a time until the wheel spins freely.

Backing off an automatic adjuster

Automatic adjusters keep the brakes in correct adjustment all the time, but if you need to remove the brake drum for any reason you may have to back off the adjuster a little to pull the drum clear.

Raise the car, support it on axle stands and remove the wheel. On some cars such as Vauxhalls you back off the adjustment by turning the two bolts on the rear of the backplate. The bolts are turned towards each other backing the shoes away from the drum. Only a little adjustment is necessary.

On other cars you will find a hole in the brake drum or the backplate, through which you can see a toothed wheel (similar to the star wheel adjuster). You can back this off using a screwdriver.

After reasssembly, you only need to operate the footbrake or handbrake to restore the proper brake adjustment. The adjuster will automatically take up the slack.

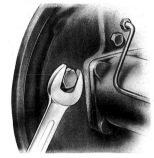

Turn the hexagonal bolts on the backplate to back the shoes off the drum.

With the shoes backed off you can now remove the brake drum and work on the components inside.

Fitting new drum brake shoes

After examining the brake shoes (see pages 65, 66, 67, 68) you may find they have worn down so much that you need to replace them.

Fitting the new shoes is exactly the reverse procedure of taking off the old ones. So, as you go along, make notes on how you dismantle the brakes.

Return springs

To take off any kind of brake shoe you have to remove the hold-down springs and the return springs. So before you start, make a note of where each spring fits and which holes in the brake shoes they fit in. This is important since the shoes may be common to several different cars and there is often more than one set of holes.

On a twin-leading shoe brake, each shoe is attached by its own return spring to the backplate. You need to detach this spring from the backplate before removing the shoe.

On a leading-and-trailing shoe brake, the springs are stretched between the pair of shoes and you can usually remove both shoes together, complete with the springs.

Reassembly tips

Before you reassemble the brakes, clean any brake dust from the drums because it can cause brake squeal. Don't breathe any in as it contains poisonous asbestos.

Before refitting the drums, make sure you have retracted any brake adjusters or the handbrake mechanism. Ensure you have fitted the shoes centrally or the drum won't fit on. Adjust them if necessary.

After refitting the drum and before adjusting the brakes (see pages 69, 70, 71, 72), press the pedal a few times to centralize the shoes.

 intermediate

Tools and materials
- ☐ Pliers
- ☐ Heavy screwdriver, adjustable spanner or shoe horn
- ☐ Piece of wire
- ☐ High-melting-point grease
- ☐ New shoes; other parts as needed
- ☐ Spanner
- ☐ Pen and paper
- ☐ Face mask

☆ Draw it

When dismantling brakes, have a pen and paper handy to draw the sometimes complicated way certain parts fit together. Vital details include which way round brake shoes fit, which holes the return springs fit into and which way round they go, the position of retaining pins and automatic adjusters, and the order in which washers are fitted.

If you own a Polaroid camera, photograph these details instead.

The parts of a drum brake

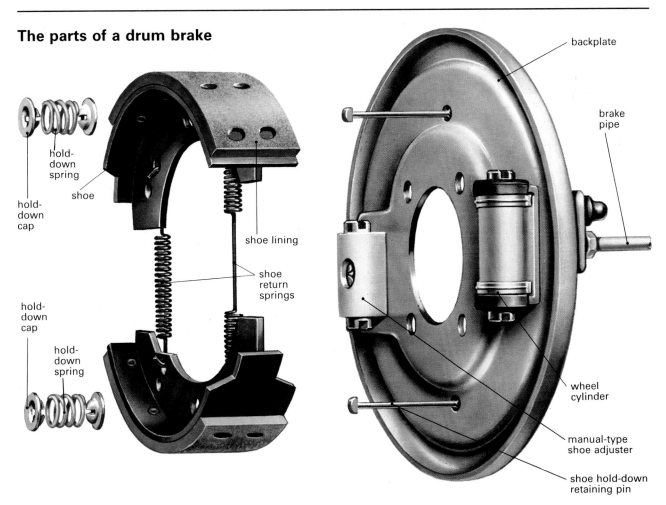

hold-down spring

hold-down cap

shoe

hold-down cap

hold-down spring

shoe lining

shoe return springs

backplate

brake pipe

wheel cylinder

manual-type shoe adjuster

shoe hold-down retaining pin

Removing and refitting brake shoes

1 To remove a coil hold-down spring, grip the edge of the cap with pliers. Push it in and turn it until the slot in the cap will pass over the head of the T-shaped pin. Remove the cap, holding the pin behind the backplate.

2 Take off the hold-down spring and pull the pin through the backplate. If it is a rear wheel, disconnect the linkage between the brake shoe and the handbrake mechanism if necessary.

3 Lever each shoe from its slot in the wheel cylinder using a heavy screwdriver or shoe horn (see sideline), trying not to damage the rubber dust cover on the cylinder. This releases the tension of the return springs.

4 You can now remove the shoes and return springs. On a twin-leading-shoe brake, unhook the springs from the backplate. On a leading-and-trailing brake, unhook the top spring then remove both shoes and the lower spring.

5 With the shoes and the return springs removed, wind some wire round the wheel cylinder to secure the piston. Clean out the abutment slots in the adjuster and lubricate them lightly with high-melting-point grease.

6 Connect the new shoes and return springs on the ground, then place one end of each shoe in its abutment slot in the adjuster. Note the lining on each shoe is offset – position the new shoes for fitting in the same way as the old.

7 Remove the wire from the wheel cylinder and lever the new shoes on to the cylinder. With rear brakes, reconnect the handbrake mechanism if necessary. Replace the hold-down pins, springs and caps in reverse order to removal.

8 Replace the drum. Fully tighten the adjuster (shown here for clarity with drum removed) with the correct tool (here a spanner) then unscrew it until the drum is able to revolve (see pages 69, 70, 71, 72). Refit the wheel.

Using a shoe horn

Once you have removed the hold-down springs you need to free the shoes from their slots in the cylinder before you can pull them off. A tool called a shoe horn makes this easier by giving you a good grip on the shoe.

Alternatively, if you don't have a shoe horn, lever the shoe away from the cylinder with a heavy screwdriver braced against a bolt on the backplate.

Another alternative to the shoe horn is to use an L-shaped adjustable spanner.

⚠ Brake dust

When working with the brakes, remember not to breathe in any of the brake dust. It contains asbestos and can be hazardous. If necessary, wear a face mask.

Two types of hold-down spring

Removing a coil spring (above, with details of the spring, right), and removing a spring clip (below, with detail, below right).

The brake shoe hold-down spring may be either a cap and coil spring assembly or a U-shaped spring clip. It fits over a T-shaped pin – one on each shoe – which passes through the backplate and the shoe.

To remove a coil hold-down spring you hold the pin from behind with a finger and turn the cap of the spring with pliers until the cap slot lines up with the pin head.

To remove a spring clip you pinch the end of the pin with pliers and turn it through 90° so that it will pass through the forked end of the spring clip.

Removing twin-leading shoes

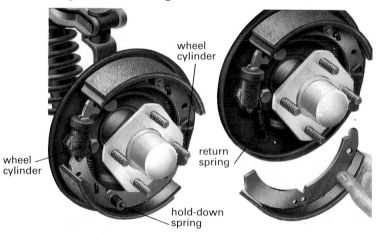

Remove the hold-down spring, lever the shoe free and pull it towards you. Once the tension on the shoe is released, you can detach the return spring and lift the shoe off. Repeat the procedure for the other shoe – note which hole the end of the spring fits into on both the shoe and the backplate.

As soon as the shoes are off, wind wire around each wheel cylinder to stop the pistons coming out. Check the return springs are not bent or rusty and that the hooked ends do not have a groove worn in them. If they do, fit new springs.

Adjusting the handbrake

If you find you are having to pull the handbrake lever up higher and higher before it takes effect, or even that the brakes do not firmly bite even when the handbrake lever is at the top of its travel, the cable has probably stretched and needs adjusting.

First check that the brake shoes are correctly adjusted (see pages 69, 70, 71, 72) – though if this were the cause of the trouble you would probably have noticed an increase in the brake pedal travel. You must not adjust the handbrake cable in an attempt to compensate for wear in the brake linings.

Types of adjuster

Depending on your make of car, there are several different types of adjuster. One type has twin cables, each connected independently to the handbrake lever and running to one of the rear brakes. The adjustment on this type is made where the cables join the lever.

The other types have a single cable running back from the handbrake and then a linkage to both rear brakes.

There are three common ways of arranging this linkage. In one, the primary cable (the one attached to

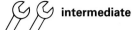 **intermediate**

Tools and materials

☐ Jack, axle stands and chocks
☐ Penetrating oil
☐ Engine oil
☐ Spanners
☐ Pliers if necessary
☐ New split pin for some types of adjuster

Single-cable and twin-cable arrangements

The way in which the handbrake lever is linked to the rear brake varies considerably from car to car. But in general there is a single cable, called the primary cable, running back from the lever and linked in some way to a secondary cable running off to the two rear brakes.

In the system shown here, the primary cable is linked to the secondary cable by a yoke held by a clevis pin.

On some cars, there are two cables joined directly to the handbrake lever (below right). These cables run back independently – one to each rear brake.

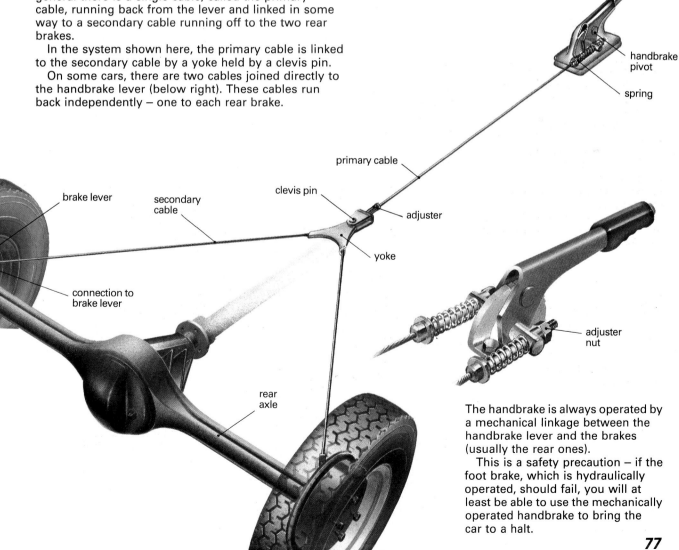

handbrake lever

handbrake pivot

spring

primary cable

clevis pin

adjuster

brake lever

secondary cable

yoke

connection to brake lever

rear axle

adjuster nut

The handbrake is always operated by a mechanical linkage between the handbrake lever and the brakes (usually the rear ones).

This is a safety precaution – if the foot brake, which is hydraulically operated, should fail, you will at least be able to use the mechanically operated handbrake to bring the car to a halt.

Adjusting at a disc brake

On most cars with all-round disc brakes, the handbrake is linked to the rear brakes, but on a few cars it operates on the front brakes.

There is usually a single adjustment on each brake to take up stretch in the handbrake cable and compensate for wear in the pads.

Support the rear or front of the car on axle stands, chock the wheels on the ground and release the handbrake.

With a large open-ended spanner, loosen by a few turns the large thin locknut on the back of the brake caliper. With a smaller open-ended spanner, turn the adjuster nut clockwise until it becomes stiff – the heel of the cast-metal lever arm should now be pressing against the back of the pad and the wheel should be hard to turn by hand.

Unscrew the adjuster nut by half to three-quarters of a turn, hold it steady and tighten up the locknut against it. Recheck the adjustment.

Relay lever and transverse rod types

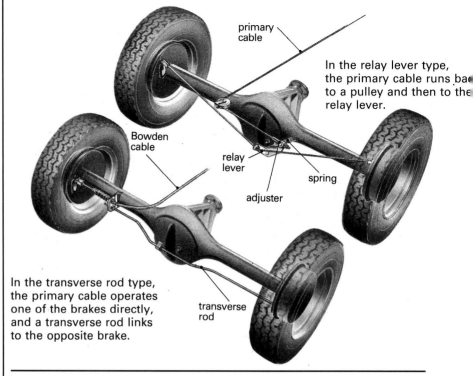

In the relay lever type, the primary cable runs back to a pulley and then to the relay lever.

In the transverse rod type, the primary cable operates one of the brakes directly, and a transverse rod links to the opposite brake.

Labels: primary cable, Bowden cable, relay lever, adjuster, spring, transverse rod

the handbrake lever) is linked via a clevis pin to a yoke. Two secondary cables run off from the yoke to the rear brakes.

Another arrangement has the primary cable running to a pulley on the rear axle. From there, the cable runs to a relay lever which operates the brakes via a secondary cable.

The third type has the primary cable running directly to one of the brake drums and the other brake drum is operated indirectly by the cable via a transverse rod connecting the two drums.

In the last of these mechanisms the primary cable is a type known as a Bowden cable, in which the cable is free to slide inside a fixed sheath. The outer sheath is threaded and has an adjusting nut on it. By turning this nut you vary the length of the sheath relative to the cable and so effectively adjust the length of the cable.

Bowden cables are also sometimes fitted as the secondary cables in the yoke-type linkage.

Disc brakes

Most cars have drum brakes at the rear and the handbrake operates directly on the brake shoes. On cars with rear disc brakes the handbrake cannot operate directly on the pads because it takes too great a force to bring them into action.

There are two ways in which car manufacturers have solved this problem. One is to fit a separate smaller set of pads, which require less force to operate and so can be worked by the handbrake. The other is to fit small brake drums to the rear wheels. These are linked to the handbrake, not to the brake's hydraulic system, so they play no part when you press the footbrake.

Getting ready

Find out from your service manual or from your dealer which type of handbrake your car has. The adjusters may be at the lever end, but more likely they will be underneath the car. If so, jack up the car, support it on axle stands and chock the front wheels.

About two hours before you plan to begin work, give all the nuts and screw threads you will be tackling a squirt of penetrating oil to loosen them.

Also use engine oil to lubricate all the pivots and linkages in the handbrake system.

Adjusting at the lever

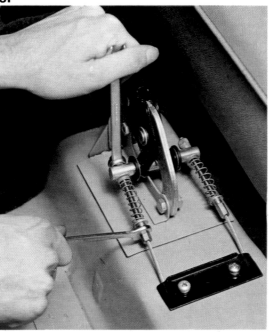

Pull away the covering or carpeting around the handbrake and find the adjusters (top left). There may be one or two cables, with just an adjuster nut or with an adjuster nut and a locknut.

If there is an adjuster nut and locknut, grip each with a spanner and screw them apart to free the locknut (above left).

Now turn the adjuster nut with a spanner while you hold the rod on the cable with a pair of pliers or a spanner to stop it turning (above right). The nut may turn smoothly or it may have a click action.

Keep adjusting until the handbrake lever can be pulled up by only three to five clicks.

If there are twin cables, adjust each by the same amount then, with the handbrake on, try turning each rear wheel. Each should offer the same resistance to turning. If they don't, readjust the cables until they do. Pull the handbrake right up and check that the wheels are fully locked. Finally, tighten the locknuts, if fitted.

Adjusting a Bowden cable

Pull the handbrake lever on three or four clicks. Loosen the locknut on the outer sheath – you may have to hold the cable itself as you do this.

Screw the locknut back a few turns along its threads on the outer sheath. Then screw the adjuster nut along the cable – in most cases, clockwise tightens it up, anti-clockwise slackens it. If yours is the odd one out, turn the other way. Turn the adjuster until you feel some resistance from the cable.

Check that the rear wheels now turn only with some effort. Readjust if necessary, then hold the adjuster nut with one spanner and tighten the locknut on to it with another.

Some designs do not need a spanner to turn the adjuster – you can turn the knurled adjuster knob by hand.

Yoke adjustment

The adjuster may be at a threaded sleeve just in front of the yoke where the secondary cables run off to the rear wheels.

Alternatively, the threaded section may run through the yoke and the adjuster nut, just inside the U-shaped part of the yoke.

Put the handbrake lever to 'off' then, without pressing the release button, pull it on three or four clicks.

There will probably be a pair of nuts, one an adjuster nut, the other a locknut.

Hold the adjuster nut with one spanner and loosen the locknut with another (left). Screw the locknut back three or four turns.

Now turn the adjuster nut clockwise until the rear wheels can be turned only with a great deal of force. Tighten the locknut.

Pull the handbrake fully on then try to turn the rear wheels. They should not move.

Transverse rod

The transverse rod has one or two adjusters depending on the design. The adjuster or adjusters are usually fitted where the primary cable and the rod join on the rear axle. An equalizing flap is fitted.

Put the handbrake into the off position then loosen the adjuster nut on the end of the primary cable (and on the transverse rod where fitted). Adjust one (or both) nuts until the equalizer flap is pointing straight back.

Apply the handbrake three to four clicks and check that the wheels are locked. If not, carry on adjusting.

☆ Final check

Once you have adjusted the handbrake cable so that the rear wheels resist your attempts to turn them with the handbrake on, put the handbrake off. Try to turn the rear wheels again. This time they should spin freely.

If they do not, the cable is now too tight and the brakes are binding on. Slacken off the adjustment and check again.

Relay lever adjustment

On some cars the single primary cable and the secondary ones are linked by a relay lever located about halfway back along the car.

The adjustment can be made to any of these three cables.

Pull the handbrake lever on one or two clicks. Find which cable has the most slack. If it is the primary, undo its locknut, turn the adjuster nut until the cable is taut, and tighten the locknut.

If the secondary cables are stretched, tighten the slacker of the two in the same way as for the primary cable, then tighten the other secondary cable. Make sure that both rear wheels offer the same resistance when you try to turn them — if they don't, adjust the appropriate secondary cable.

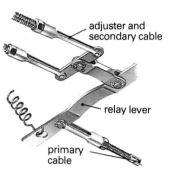

adjuster and secondary cable

relay lever

primary cable

Backplate adjustment

On some cars the adjustment is made to a fork at the end of a rod or cable just before the backplate. The fork is held to an operating lever on the backplate by a clevis pin.

Take out the split pin holding the clevis pin in place (above right), and remove the clevis pin.

Pull the handbrake on two notches, then loosen the locknut and screw back the adjuster nut (right)

until the clevis pin holes in the fork are just in line with the hole in the operating lever.

Tighten the locknut, fit the fork over the operating lever, replace the clevis pin and secure it with a new split pin.

Adjusting the primary cable at the relay lever

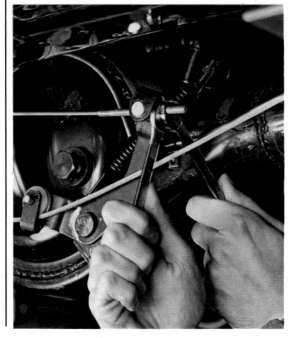

On some cars the relay lever, instead of being halfway back along the car (see top of page), lies on the rear axle.

In this case the adjustment is made on the primary cable where it meets the relay lever.

Use two spanners, one on the locknut and one on the adjuster nut. Loosen the locknut and turn the adjuster nut to tighten up the cable.

Check that the rear wheels can be turned only with some effort, then, holding the adjusting nut in place with a spanner, tighten up the locknut.

Adjusting a disc handbrake

Most cars are still fitted with drums on the back wheels with the handbrake operating directly on the brake shoes by a simple mechanical linkage.

High-quality, high-performance cars, however, often have disc brakes on the rear as well as the front wheels. With all-round disc brakes, it is very difficult to operate the rear brake pads by a mechanical linkage from the handbrake. So some manufacturers have come up with a different handbrake mechanism.

Auxiliary drum

The most common type of disc handbrake mechanism is fitted to cars such as the pre-Fiat Lancias, Jaguars, Porsches, BMWs and Volvos.

This type of handbrake consists of separate brake shoes, not pads, and works like a normal drum brake except that the drum is formed by the inner surface of the centre of the brake disc. The brake shoes are fitted with friction material just like a normal brake shoe, so they wear out over a period and need renewing. Fitting new shoes to this type of handbrake can be difficult, so refer to your garage or manual.

Check cable

If you are having problems with the handbrake, the first job is to check that the cable has not become frayed, seized or detached underneath the car.

Jack up the rear of the car and place it safely on axle stands. Follow the cable back from the handbrake lever, looking for signs of damage. Get a friend to operate the hand-

basic

Tools and materials
☐ Jack and axle stands
☐ Spanners and sockets
☐ Penetrating oil
☐ Screwdrivers

☆ Cable problems
If you find the handbrake cable is still stiff even after you've lubricated and adjusted it, then the chances are that it is seized or damaged inside its outer sheath.

The only solution is to fit a new handbrake cable.

Don't leave it for long – if the cable sticks even slightly on, the handbrake shoes will rub on the drum face and wear down very rapidly.

Drum within disc
The most common handbrake layout used on a four-wheel disc brake system has a small auxiliary drum brake mounted inside the brake disc.

A pair of brake shoes, much the same as those in a normal rear drum brake, are moved outwards by the operation of the handbrake lever. They press against a 'drum' formed by the inner surface of the centre of the brake disc.

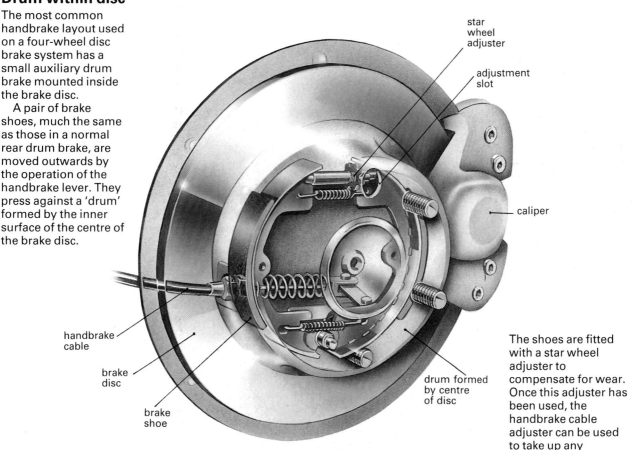

star wheel adjuster

adjustment slot

caliper

handbrake cable

brake disc

brake shoe

drum formed by centre of disc

The shoes are fitted with a star wheel adjuster to compensate for wear. Once this adjuster has been used, the handbrake cable adjuster can be used to take up any remaining slack.

Checking and adjusting the shoes

Rotate the brake disc and look through the adjustment slot to check each brake shoe in turn (**1**). If there is enough lining left, use a screwdriver to turn the star wheel adjuster (**2**) until the wheel is locked. Back off the adjuster half a turn.

To adjust the cable, use the adjuster nut at the U-shaped yoke (**3**) or on the primary cable or rod (**4**).

1 Examine each brake shoe for wear.

2 If the shoes are not too worn, adjust them with the star wheel adjuster.

3 Then adjust the cable, either at the yoke . . .

4 . . . or at the primary cable or rod.

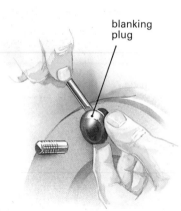

blanking plug

Adjustment slot

The adjustment slot, through which you check the handbrake shoe linings and turn the star wheel adjuster, may be sealed by a blanking plug. This is usually made of rubber or plastic and can be readily prised out with a screwdriver (above).

brake while you watch for any lost movement. If any operating levers appear to be stiff, squirt the pivot points with penetrating oil.

Check shoes

Having established that the cable is in good condition, you should next check the adjustment. It is best to consider handbrake adjustment on an all-disc system in two parts. First you have to adjust the brake mechanism itself and second you adjust the handbrake cable.

Find the handbrake cable adjuster and slacken it right off. Make sure that the cable seats properly where it passes through the backplate of the brake mechanism.

Then find the adjustment access slot, which is on the perimeter of the brake drum part of the disc assembly. It may have a blanking plug in it. Turn the brake disc so that you can view the handbrake shoes – there should be at least $\frac{1}{12}$in (2mm) of lining material left.

Star wheel adjuster

Assuming the shoes are all right, look for the star wheel adjuster.

This is usually fitted at the six o'clock position. Give the star wheel adjuster and its surrounding area a squirt of penetrating oil so that it moves more easily.

Turn the star wheel adjuster with a short heavy screwdriver by resting the screwdriver on the edge of the slot and levering against the arms of the star wheel. Turn the wheel until the rear disc is locked in position and you cannot move it by hand. Then slacken off the star wheel by half a turn – you can judge this roughly by counting off four arms. Adjust the other side in the same way.

Adjust cable

In most cases the cable adjuster is under the car and is the same as that on a typical drum handbrake. The most common has the adjuster located at a U-shaped yoke as shown on page 79.

To adjust the cable, slacken off the locknut and run the adjuster itself along the thread in the direction required to slacken or tighten the cable. Then pull the handbrake on two or three clicks, and the handbrake should lock the rear discs.

Bleeding the brakes

The foot brake is operated hydraulically – unlike the handbrake, which is mechanical. When you put your foot on the brake, fluid from the brake master reservoir is forced out and along the brake pipes to the piston (or pistons) inside the brake itself.

The fluid causes the pistons to push on either the brake shoes (in a drum brake) or the brake pads (in a disc brake), which in turn slow down the car.

Ageing fluid

Brake fluid is hygroscopic; it absorbs moisture from the atmosphere over a period of time, and this can reduce the car's braking power. When you brake, the rubbing of the brake linings against the disc or drum causes the fluid to become hotter and hotter.

While this makes no difference to new brake fluid because it has a very high boiling point, the moisture present in older fluid turns to steam and forms bubbles in the fluid. Because these bubbles are compressible (unlike brake fluid), the brake pedal feels 'spongy' when you press it. In very severe cases so much air forms that the brakes may fail completely.

The brake pedal may also feel spongy if there is a leak in the braking system that is letting air get into the fluid.

In either case, you need to replace completely the old brake fluid with new fluid, thereby removing the unwanted air bubbles and moisture at the same time. This is known as bleeding the brakes. You do this by opening special bleed nipples (effectively valves) on each brake and letting out the old fluid through them, while at the same time topping up the master cylinder reservoir with fresh fluid.

Even if your brakes don't feel spongy you should still replace the brake fluid every two years.

First checks

Before you start to bleed the brakes, first check there are no leaks in the system that are causing the brakes to feel spongy. Examine the brake pipes and the seals for

intermediate

Tools and materials

☐ Jack, axle stands and chocks
☐ Wire brush
☐ Ring spanners
☐ Clear plastic tubing, about 2ft (60cm) in length
☐ Jam jar or other glass container
☐ Penetrating oil, if necessary
☐ Fresh brake fluid
☐ New nipple dust covers, if necessary
☐ Brake bleeding kit, if required

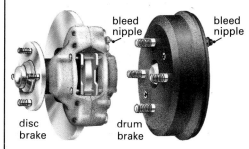

disc brake   drum brake

Finding the bleed nipple

On a disc brake the bleed nipple is on the side of the caliper. On a drum brake it is on the backplate.

Dual-circuit braking system

This has two separate circuits, each connected to the master cylinder. On some cars, the two circuits serve the front and rear wheels respectively, but on others the split is diagonal – each circuit serving one front and one rear wheel – or has some other configuration.

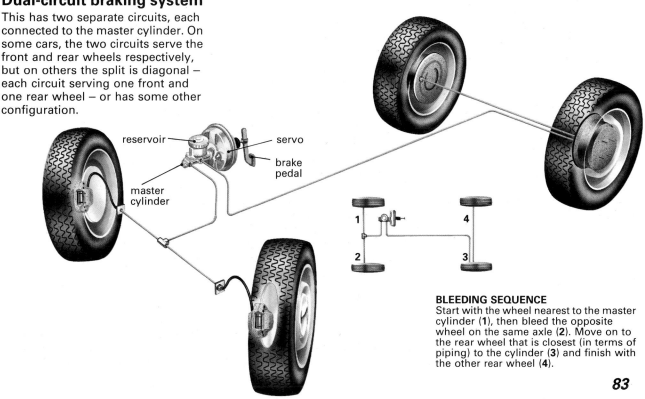

reservoir   servo

master cylinder   brake pedal

BLEEDING SEQUENCE
Start with the wheel nearest to the master cylinder (**1**), then bleed the opposite wheel on the same axle (**2**). Move on to the rear wheel that is closest (in terms of piping) to the cylinder (**3**) and finish with the other rear wheel (**4**).

☆ On your own

You can buy a special bleed tube with a non-return valve so you can do this job on your own. The valve stops any fluid being drawn back up the tube from the jam jar, so you don't need to tighten the bleed nipple every time the brake pedal is pressed down. You can press the brake pedal yourself, knowing that there's no danger of air getting back into the system.

The only problem is that you cannot see the tube and so cannot tell when the air has been bled out. For one-man brake bleeding that allows you to watch the tube, see the sideline on the next sheet.

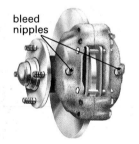

Four-piston bleed nipples

On disc brakes with four pistons, there are usually two bleed nipples, one for each pair of pistons. These nipples both need to be bled.

On the BL Metro, the four-piston system has three bleed nipples.

Single-circuit braking systems

These have a single pipe from the master cylinder to all four brakes.

In this case, you start the bleeding process at the wheel furthest from the cylinder (**1**) and end at the nearest (**4**).

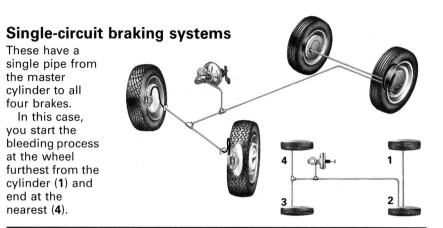

signs of leaking (look for signs of brake fluid on the outside).

If you discover any leaks, fix them before you bleed the brakes or the problem will recur.

Next, find out what type of braking system your car has by looking in your handbook or asking your dealer. It may be single circuit, in which a single pipe leads from the master cylinder to the brakes, or (more likely) it may be dual circuit, in which there are two pipes leading from the master cylinder – each one operating half the braking system. Some dual circuits are split so that one half operates the front brakes and one half the rear. Or the circuit may be split diagonally.

If your car has a dual-circuit system, you need to know how the circuit is split and also whether the system has front disc brakes with four pistons per caliper.

The type of braking system your car has affects the order in which you bleed the brakes. On a single-circuit system, you start with the brake furthest from the master cylinder and end on the one nearest to it. On a dual-circuit, two-piston

system, the bleeding is done in two separate operations because there are two circuits. Start with the wheel nearest to the master cylinder in each case.

On a dual-circuit, four-piston system you start with the rear brake furthest from the master cylinder, then bleed the front-caliper pistons on the same side of the car. Repeat this sequence for the brakes on the other side.

Cars with servo-assisted brakes may have a bleed nipple on the servo unit. If so, start with that, then continue with the appropriate sequence.

Prepare the car

You can often reach the bleed nipples with the road wheels in place, but the job is easier if you remove the wheels first.

Jack up the car and support all four wheels on axle stands. If you cannot do this, do one wheel at a time. Find each bleed nipple (its position depends on whether the brake is disc or drum), and clean it with a wire brush.

Four-piston systems

This is a dual-circuit system. The front brakes have two pipes leading to them and two nipples.

You bleed the brakes on one half of the car (**1-3**), then on the other (**4-6**), in each case starting with the rear wheel.

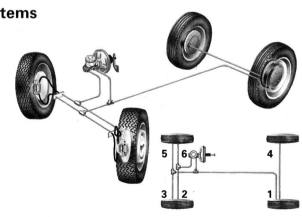

Open the nipple

The method of bleeding is the same whether your car has disc brakes, drum brakes or a mixture. If you have a mixture of brakes on your car, however, the nipple sizes may be different, so make sure you have the correct size ring spanner for each one.

If a dust cover is fitted, remove it. Place the spanner over the nipple, but don't turn it yet. Attach a length (about 2ft/60cm long) of clear plastic tubing to the nipple. It should be an airtight fit.

Put the free end of the tube into a clean glass container, such as an old jam jar, and pour into the jar enough fresh brake fluid so that the end of the tube is submerged in at least ½in (13mm) of fluid.

Now open the bleed nipple. Take care – it is made of soft metal. If it refuses to budge, apply penetrating oil to the thread and leave it for a few minutes.

Loosen the nipple for about half a turn and leave the spanner in place. Brake fluid should begin to flow down the tube and into the jar. If it does not, the nipple may be blocked. If so, see overleaf.

Pump the brakes

When the brake fluid is flowing, ask your helper to pump the brake pedal (to force the fluid out) while you watch the fluid run through the clear tubing. Keep checking the level of fluid in the master cylinder and keep it topped up.

The way the brake pedal is pumped depends on the type of master cylinder your car has. There are two types – aluminium-bodied centre-valve (CV) type or cast-iron compression-barrel (CB) type.

With the CV type, your helper

The bleeding process

First clean off dirt from the nipple (**1**). Then fit a ring spanner over the nipple and attach the bleed tube (**2**). Open the nipple with the spanner and allow the fluid to flow out. Close the nipple with the spanner and remove the tube (**3**).

ean the nipple a wire brush.

fter bleeding, ove the ner and the

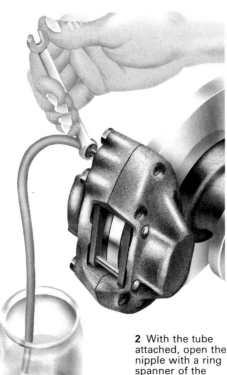

2 With the tube attached, open the nipple with a ring spanner of the correct size.

⚠ Spillage

Take great care not to spill any brake fluid on to your car bodywork. It is extremely corrosive and will start to eat its way through within seconds.

If you do spill any, hose it off immediately, and wipe the area with a clean rag. Wash your hands thoroughly afterwards.

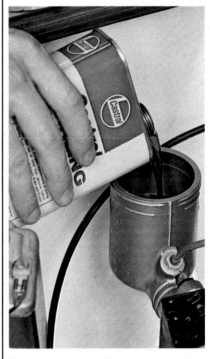

Topping up the reservoir

Keep the reservoir well topped up with brake fluid while you do this job. Check with your car handbook to see what type of fluid you should use for your car; if you top up with the wrong fluid you may permanently damage the braking system.

Also make sure that you don't shake the can or leave the fluid exposed to air for more than a brief period. If you do, air bubbles will enter the fluid and so get back into the system again.

☆ Overnight

If the pedal still feels spongy after you've bled the brakes, then you could try bleeding them overnight.

To do this, you need to jam a piece of wood against the pedal to hold it down permanently. This will allow any bubbles in the fluid to work their way overnight up to the master cylinder reservoir and so escape from the system.

Pressure bleeder

To help you bleed the brakes you can buy a kit that works off the pressure in your spare tyre.

Set up the kit as specified in the instructions, using the reservoir cap that matches your brake fluid reservoir. Fill the bottle on the kit to the correct level. Let the spare tyre down to the pressure in the instructions and connect the valve on the kit to the tyre.

Now go to the wheel to be bled, and fit the tube and spanner in the normal way. Immerse the end of the tube in brake fluid. Open the bleed nipple and let the pressure force the old fluid out.

Although the fluid bottle should have ample capacity for most braking systems, keep an eye on the level all the time.

Which cylinder?

centre-valve (CV)
master cylinder

compression-barrel (CB)
master cylinder

Check your master cylinder against the ones shown here to find out which type your car has.

The main differences are in the shape of the reservoir – the CB reservoir is much squatter than the CV one – and in the material the cylinder is made from. CVs are generally made from aluminium and CBs from cast iron.

pushes the pedal down fully, gives it three short, quick strokes near the bottom of its travel and releases it fully. This is repeated straightaway and continued until no more air comes from the nipple.

With the CB type, your helper pushes the pedal down fully to the floor, then lets it rise slowly. Wait for three or four seconds, then have your helper repeat this until all the air is expelled.

With either type, once all the air has been expelled, tell your helper to pump the brake pedal twice more, then to keep the pedal depressed while you close the nipple by tightening it with a spanner.

When you have finished, remove the tubing and spanner. Refit the dust cap on to the nipple – if there wasn't one originally, buy one and fit it now. Replace the road wheel and move on to the next nipple in the sequence.

If you are simply replacing the old fluid with new, pump the foot brake six times for each nipple. This is enough to pump out the old fluid and replace it with fresh.

Check the result

When you have bled all the brakes, apply hard foot pressure to the brake pedal. It should no longer feel spongy – if it does, there is still air trapped in the system and it needs further bleeding.

To test the brakes on the road, drive to a quiet stretch and wait until there is no traffic. Drive slowly for a short distance and press the brake pedal as you would normally. Do the same driving at normal speed. The car should pull up quickly and in a straight line in each case, and the pedal should not feel spongy.

Repeat the test a few more times. If the sponginess returns to the brakes, there is still some old fluid or air in the system and you will have to bleed the brakes again. Make sure that you were using the correct sequence for your type of braking system – whether single or dual circuit – and that your helper was pumping the brakes correctly.

Curing a blocked bleed nipple

brake-hose
clamp

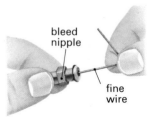

bleed
nipple

fine
wire

If bleeding does not begin when you open a bleed nipple, it is probably blocked.

To clear the blockage, first seal the hose leading to that brake with a brake-hose clamp. Next, remove the plastic tube you have just attached and unscrew the nipple. Poke the nipple clear with a piece of stiff thin wire and replace the nipple tightly. Then remove the clamp. Fluid should now flow through it.

Finding and fixing brake leaks

Usually the first signs of a leak in the braking system are that the pedal goes down further than normal or it begins to feel 'spongy'. In either case, you need to find the cause of the problem immediately, otherwise your brakes could fail.

Level check

First check the fluid level in the master cylinder reservoir. It should be right up to the maximum – if it is low, top it up.

If the level goes down soon after topping up, then there is a leak in the system and you must check all the components to find it.

Before you start, jack the car up and support it on axle stands.

Master cylinder

If the rubber seals on the brake master cylinder have failed, fluid can leak on to the brake pedal.

Put your hand up behind the brake pedal and check the rod for signs of hydraulic fluid. Also squeeze the rubber dust cover where the rod disappears into the master cylinder to see if fluid oozes out.

Pipe and hoses

Examine the metal pipes where they come out of the master cylinder – they should be dry. If the joint is weeping you can usually cure it by tightening it slightly with a spanner.

If the unions are dry, follow the brake pipes along looking for signs of rusting. Check every union and pipe for leaks.

Follow each pipe along to the front brakes. Check the unions where they join the hoses very carefully. Also check the condition of the hose itself. Bend the hose right back as far as it will go against the metal end sections. This will reveal any splits which are not visible with the hose straight. Also look for signs of the hose chafing on other components – fit a new hose if

⚲ basic

Tools and materials
☐ Jack, axle stands and chocks
☐ Spanners
☐ Wire brush
☐ Fresh brake fluid for topping up

Caliper check

Inspect the caliper pistons to see if any show signs of a fluid leak. If there is a leak, the piston seals have worn and the calipers need replacing or overhauling. You may be able to pull back the dust cover (above) to have a look.

Inspecting for leaks

Check the rubber seals on the wheel cylinder inside the brake drum.

A leak can occur at any of several points in a hydraulic brake system. If you suspect a leak, check the parts of the system shown here, one by one, until you find the cause.

servo unit, master cylinder and reservoir

brake pedal

brake caliper

metal brake pipe

flexible brake hose

Steps to tracing a leak in the braking system

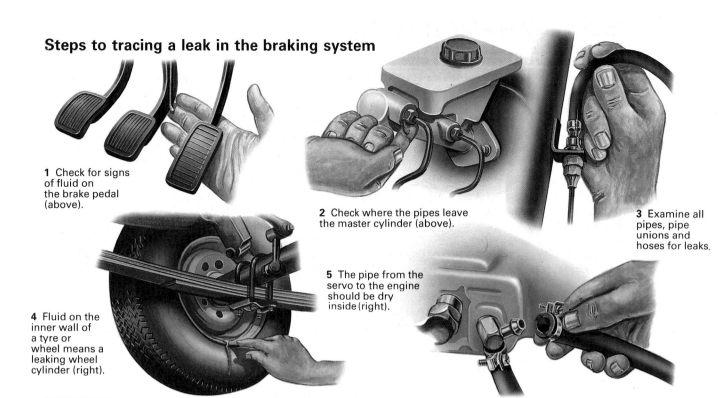

1 Check for signs of fluid on the brake pedal (above).

2 Check where the pipes leave the master cylinder (above).

3 Examine all pipes, pipe unions and hoses for leaks.

4 Fluid on the inner wall of a tyre or wheel means a leaking wheel cylinder (right).

5 The pipe from the servo to the engine should be dry inside (right).

☆ A helping foot

When you are inspecting for brake leaks, it helps to have a friend pump the brakes while you check. The extra pressure this creates in the braking system forces out fluid at any leaks, making them much easier to see.

☆ Copper pipes

If you find a leaking brake pipe, it can be a good idea to replace it with one made from copper alloy rather than steel. Copper pipes last much longer because they don't rust, but they are more expensive.

it is damaged in any way.

Finally get a helper to press hard on the brake pedal – if the hose swells at all, it is in a very dangerous condition – it could burst and leave you without brakes. Replace it immediately.

Rear pipes

If the front brake pipes seem all right, next check the ones running to the rear. With the car supported on stands, go underneath and check the metal pipes along the whole of their length.

Again check all the unions for leaks, and examine the metal pipes for rust. Use a wire brush to clean up any suspect area. If the rust has pitted the pipe it needs renewing. Bend flexible hoses to check them for splits.

Some cars are fitted with a pressure limiter to stop the rear brakes locking up in an emergency stop. Check that there are no signs of fluid leaking out of it.

Wheel cylinders

A very bad leak from a wheel cylinder is often revealed by fluid stains on the inner wall of the tyre or wheel. Furthermore, the brakes will have a tendency to pull to the

opposite side to where the leak is.

To check the wheel cylinder you must first remove the brake drum (see pages 65, 66, 67, 68). A serious leak will be obvious – the whole of the inside of the drum and the brake shoes will be covered in a slimy mixture of fluid and brake dust.

If no leak is visible, use your fingers or a screwdriver to carefully prise back the rubber dust cover from the wheel cylinder. The inside should be totally dry.

Leaks from the brake calipers are less common than from wheel cylinders, but they do happen. To check, identify the hydraulic piston part of the caliper. Depending on the type of car there may be one, two, three or four pistons in each caliper. Look carefully to see if any are leaking.

Brake servo

If you still haven't found the leak and your car has an indirect-acting brake servo, then the seals inside this may have failed.

Undo the rubber pipe from the servo where it attaches to the engine and examine the inside of it. If the pipe is wet with brake fluid, the servo is leaking and the cylinder seals must be replaced.

Renewing a drum-brake wheel cylinder

Whenever you check the shoes on your drum brakes you should also inspect the wheel cylinders housing the pistons. The piston seals can deteriorate with age – the rubber naturally swells after a time and no longer seals properly. The cylinder then starts to leak fluid, which runs on to the shoes and affects their braking power.

To check for a leaking wheel cylinder, peel back the dust covers on each end. The outside of the cylinder and piston should be dry underneath. If there is any sign of fluid, the cylinder is leaking and needs to be replaced.

Clean up

First loosen the appropriate wheel nuts and jack up the rear of the car (drum brakes are usually fitted only to the rear wheels rather than both front and rear). Support the rear of the car on axle stands. Take off the wheel.

Remove the drum and brake shoes (see pages 65 to 76). Use a wire brush to clean around the backplate, the brake pipe or hose union or unions and nut or nuts. Make sure you remove any flakes of rust and also any grit from the area. If you don't, they may enter the braking system while you are working on it and cause serious damage. Take care not to breathe in any asbestos from the brake shoes while you are doing this – it is advisable to wear a face mask.

Before you start work on the wheel cylinder, take off the master cylinder reservoir cap if possible,

⚒⚒ **intermediate**

Tools and materials
- [ ] Jack, axle stands and chocks
- [ ] Wire brush
- [ ] Face mask
- [ ] Plastic sheet
- [ ] Brake hose clamps
- [ ] Spanners and screwdrivers
- [ ] Plastic bag and rubber band
- [ ] New cylinder kit, including gasket, clips and bleed nipple as necessary
- [ ] Drift
- [ ] Hammer
- [ ] Penetrating oil, if needed
- [ ] Self-locking pliers, if needed
- [ ] New brake fluid

☆ Save on fluid
Before you begin work, unscrew the master cylinder reservoir, cover its top with a sheet of plastic, then screw the top back on again. This will hold much of the fluid in the reservoir instead of it pouring out when you come to undo the brake pipe or hose.

⚠ Asbestos
Most drum brake shoes are made of asbestos, which is poisonous. So when you clean around the cylinder wear a face mask to stop you inhaling any of the asbestos dust.

Types of drum brake

This drum brake has a leading-and-trailing shoe arrangement operated by a single cylinder, which may be fixed or sliding. An alternative arrangement is to have twin leading shoes, each with its own cylinder.

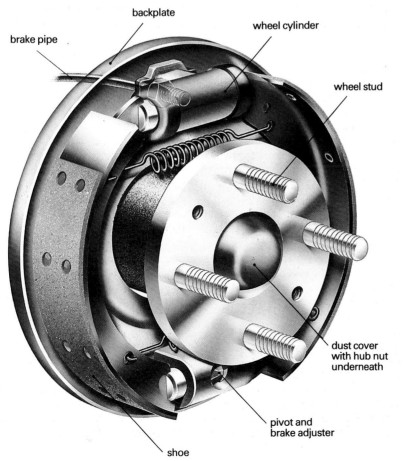

backplate
brake pipe
wheel cylinder
wheel stud
dust cover with hub nut underneath
pivot and brake adjuster
shoe

⚠ Handbrake problems

If your car has a sliding wheel cylinder, you may have to disconnect and remove the operating lever that is connected to the handbrake.

Find the end of the lever that connects to the handbrake linkage. It will be attached by a clevis pin secured by a split pin. Bend the ends of the split pin straight, then pull it out with pliers.

Push out the clevis pin using a screwdriver, and pull the handbrake cable away from the lever. You can now pull the lever out of the brake backplate (or the wheel cylinder on some designs) – it comes out from the front side. Now carry on and remove the cylinder.

Clamp the hose

Before you disconnect a brake hose, seal it off with a clamp to reduce the loss of brake fluid from it.

In the case of a metal pipe, which cannot be clamped, follow it back away from the brake until you see it joining a flexible hose. Clamp that hose.

place a sheet of plastic over the reservoir and screw the cap back on. This blocks the breather hole in the cap and minimizes the loss of brake fluid when you come to undo the brake pipe or hose.

Undo metal pipe

The wheel cylinder is fed with brake fluid from the master cylinder by either a metal pipe or a flexible hose. Check to see which one your car has.

If the brake has a metal pipe, follow it back away from the brake until you see it meeting a flexible hose. Clamp the flexible hose tightly with a special clamp or a pair of

Removing the cylinder

Wire brush the whole area (**1**), then undo the union holding the brake pipe (**2**). Undo the bolts (**3**) or clips (**4**) holding the cylinder on.

1 Use a wire brush to remove all rust and dirt from the backplate, pipe union and securing bolts, nuts or clips (right).

2 Undo the union holding the pipe to the cylinder (left).

3 Undo the bolts holding the cylinder to the backplate. There may be two bolts (as right) or one.

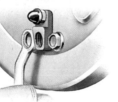

spring clip

Mole grips padded with a rag to prevent damage. This will prevent loss of brake fluid when you come to undo the pipe.

Now slacken off the union with a spanner. If you can undo the union completely, do so and pull the pipe back out of the way of the cylinder. If you cannot undo the union, leave the pipe attached to the cylinder for the time being, then try again to take it off once you have released the cylinder.

Once the pipe is off, seal its end with a small plastic bag tightly secured with a rubber band to stop dirt getting in.

Note that some cars have two brake pipes on one of their cylinders –

E-clip

4 The cylinder may be held on by an E-clip (above) or in the case of a sliding cylinder by a pair of spring clips (left).

Securing the pipe

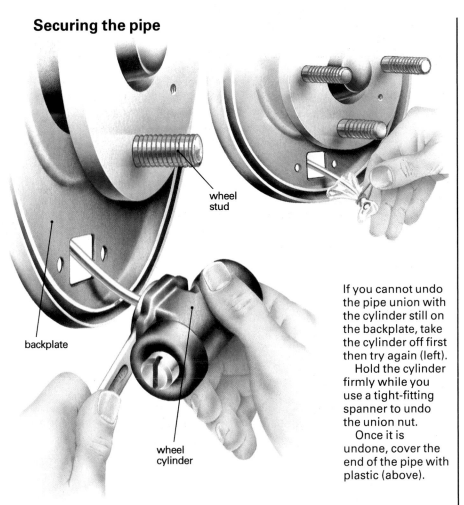

wheel
stud

backplate

wheel
cylinder

If you cannot undo the pipe union with the cylinder still on the backplate, take the cylinder off first then try again (left).

Hold the cylinder firmly while you use a tight-fitting spanner to undo the union nut.

Once it is undone, cover the end of the pipe with plastic (above).

Removing the bleed nipple

On some cars the bleed nipple is too large to get through the hole in the backplate provided for the wheel cylinder. If so, you will have to take it off using a spanner.

Save the nipple's dust cover (above) so you can refit it to the new bleed nipple supplied with your cylinder kit.

brake pipe

brake pipe

Double union cylinders

You may find that the cylinder has two unions, both of which have to be undone before you can remove the cylinder. On some cars this is because one of the rear cylinders feeds the other with brake fluid, instead of that other cylinder being supplied directly from the master cylinder. So one union connects to the master cylinder and the other leads to the cylinder on the opposite wheel.

This arrangement is found on some Cortinas, Escorts, Marinas, Hillman Avengers and the Humber Sceptre, as well as other cars.

The double union also occurs on brakes with two leading shoes, in which there is a bridge pipe from one wheel cylinder to the other.

---

one pipe comes from the master cylinder, the other feeds brake fluid to the opposite brake cylinder.

Undo flexible hose

If your brake has a flexible hose, first clamp it (see above) to prevent fluid loss. Then slacken off its metal end where it meets the backplate (the end has flats on it for this purpose).

You cannot, at this stage, undo the hose completely because it would simply twist round and round as you undid the union. Instead, you have two choices.

You can wait until you have taken off the cylinder and then spin the cylinder off the end of the hose – but to do this the hole in the backplate has to be big enough for the hose union to pass through it.

The alternative method is to follow the hose back until you find the point where it meets a metal pipe leading to the master cylinder. Undo the union between the two, release the locknut and then spin the hose off at the brake end. You will lose some brake fluid using this method because you can't clamp the metal pipe, so put a container underneath to catch it. Discard the fluid – do not reuse it.

Again, seal the end of the hose or pipe with a plastic bag.

Remove cylinder

The wheel cylinder is held on by nuts, bolts or clips. If held on by nuts or bolts, there will be one or two of them – undo them. The cylinder may have a projection that fits into a hole in the backplate to stop it from turning when you brake. Carefully wiggle the cylinder free from this and lift it away.

There may be a gasket between the cylinder and the backplate. Renew this – a new one is usually supplied with the new cylinder.

You may also find that you have to take off the bleed nipple before you can remove the cylinder, though on most cars this nipple comes off attached to the wheel cylinder. The nipple is fitted with flats, so if you have to take it off you simply undo it with a spanner. Make sure you fit a new bleed nipple with the new cylinder – it should come with the kit.

E-clip cylinders

Some wheel cylinders are secured by clips. Fixed cylinders have an E-clip; sliding cylinders have a pair of interlocking spring clips.

The E-clip is shaped like a capital 'E' with rounded arms – the middle arm of the 'E' is no more than a lug. A large part of the cylinder fits through a hole in the backplate and is held there by this clip, which fits round a groove in the projecting part of the cylinder body.

Prise off the clip using a screwdriver and discard it. A new one should be supplied with your new cylinder.

Sliding cylinder

The base of a sliding cylinder projects through a keyhole slot in the backplate, in which it is free to slide. The base is held to the backplate either by two spring clips or by two non-springy clips and a spring plate. There is usually a dust cover to ensure that the cylinder can slide freely in its slot without dirt getting in.

Pull back the dust cover. If there are two spring clips, they will often consist of an outer clip with two lugs and an inner clip with two matching holes. Use a drift (or screwdriver) and hammer to force the two clips apart. Often the spring clips are inserted from opposite sides. After you have removed one, push the second one in the other direction.

If there are two non-springy clips under a spring plate, slide the clip next to the handbrake linkage as far towards the linkage as possible. Push the other clip in the same direction until you can ease its end under the spring plate. Push the first clip to lift the spring off the second clip. Then pull the second clip free and lift off the plate and the first clip.

To remove the cylinder, slide it into the larger part of its keyhole slot and lift it free. Clean both sides of the slot and smear them with a little brake grease.

Pipe/hose removal

If the pipe or flexible hose is still attached to the cylinder, you should now be able to remove it following the steps given above.

Use penetrating oil to release a stubborn union: leave it to soak in for a while. Take care not to twist a metal pipe when you undo it. Also, brake pipe union nuts are soft, so use a tight-fitting spanner to undo it. A particularly difficult nut may need self-locking pliers (Mole grips) to start it.

Once the pipe or hose is off, seal its end with a plastic bag secured with a rubber band.

Reassembly

Fit a new gasket between the new cylinder and the backplate, if necessary. Then, for a bolt-on cylinder, fit it hand-tight to the backplate and refit the pipe, pipes or hose union by hand. Once the pipe or hose fits properly, tighten up all the unions, nuts or bolts with a spanner.

For a clip-on cylinder, refit the pipe or hose first (if they are long enough to allow you to do this), then position the cylinder on the backplate and fit the clips by knocking them in place with a hammer and drift. For a sliding cylinder make sure the dust cover fits properly so no dirt or water spray can enter and cause the cylinder to seize.

Make sure that the handbrake lever is correctly located in the cylinder or the backplate and then reconnect the cable.

Refit the brake shoes and drum, top up the master reservoir with fresh fluid and bleed the brakes (see pages 83, 84, 85, 86).

Fitting the new cylinder

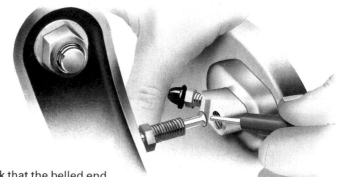

1 Check that the belled end of the brake pipe or hose is clean and undamaged.

2 For a clip-on cylinder, screw on the pipe then secure the cylinder. Fix a bolt-on cylinder loosely to the backplate, then the pipe, then tighten up.

Master cylinder and servo replacement

When you brake, fluid from the brake master cylinder is forced along the brake hoses to the brakes themselves. If this cylinder develops a leak it needs to be replaced.

Most cars today are fitted with a brake servo unit that helps to reduce the amount of pressure you have to put on the foot brake, and so makes braking easier. A brake servo unit should be replaced if it is leaking or faulty – you can tell a servo is faulty when the brake pedal is hard to push down and you have eliminated all other possible causes.

These sheets cover replacing a master cylinder and a direct-acting servo – the most common kind – along with its air filter. A direct-acting servo is mounted immediately behind the master cylinder.

Drain the system

It is generally better to drain the brake system of all brake fluid before you start removing the master cylinder. This is done by opening the bleed nipples on each brake and then pumping the pedal. For details of how to do this, and the order in which you open the nipples, see pages 83, 84, 85, 86.

Catch the old brake fluid in a jar and discard it – when you come to refill the system you should take the opportunity to use fresh fluid.

In most cases you can gain access to the master cylinder without problems, but on the Hillman Imp the fuel tank gets in the way and must be removed first.

Remove cylinder

Uncouple the metal brake pipes leading from the master cylinder. The unions are made of soft metal, so use a correctly sized spanner to avoid damaging them. Seal the end of each pipe to stop any remaining brake fluid from dripping out and damaging the paintwork. Discon-

 advanced

Tools and materials

☐ Screwdrivers and spanners
☐ Old jam jar
☐ Rags
☐ New master cylinder and/or new servo, as needed
☐ Fresh brake fluid
☐ Brake bleeding equipment
☐ Replacement split pin, gasket, hose clips and servo air filter, as needed
☐ Craft knife

☆ Finding the cylinder

On most cars the brake master cylinder is under the bonnet or, in rear-engined cars, in the front luggage compartment.

But on some cars, such as the Fiat 127, the master cylinder is inside the car just above the pedals.

The brake master cylinder and servo

Labels: breather hole, reservoir cap, servo, air filter gaiter, brake pedal, clevis pin, pushrod to pedal, brake fluid reservoir, master cylinder, non-return valve, brake pipes, vacuum hose to manifold

Brake fluid is stored in a reservoir that sits on top of the master cylinder.

The master cylinder shown here has two brake lines leading from it to serve a dual-circuit braking system.

The servo is connected to the engine inlet manifold to provide the vacuum assistance it needs to work the master cylinder. A non-return valve is fitted to the vacuum hose leading to the manifold.

nect any electrical leads, such as those to the fluid-level warning light or the brake light switch. You may also have to disconnect other linkages that get in the way, such as the choke or throttle cables.

The master cylinder is generally secured to the brake servo by two nuts and studs, or by two nuts and bolts. Sometimes there is also a steady bracket holding it to the inside of the front wing. On VW Beetles, the master cylinder is inside the front luggage compartment and is secured by bolts that you reach from inside the front wheel arch. You have to remove the wheel to get at the nuts.

Whatever your type of cylinder, undo the nuts or bolts holding it in place. Discard or overhaul the old cylinder as necessary and fit the new one but leave the mounting bolts a little loose. Screw the brake pipe unions into the cylinder by hand – take care because they are easily cross-threaded. Once the pipes are in, fully tighten the cylinder mounting bolts, then the pipe unions.

If you originally emptied the brake reservoir, fill it up with fresh brake fluid. Then, whatever the type of cylinder, bleed the brakes to get rid of air (see pages 83, 84, 85, 86). Top up the reservoir again to the maximum level with fresh brake fluid once you've bled the brakes. Replace the cylinder cap and wipe off any excess fluid.

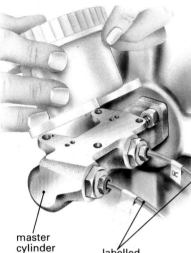

master cylinder

labelled brake pipes

Detachable reservoir

On some cars the fluid reservoir can be removed while it is still full of fluid. First seal the breather hole in the reservoir cap, then lift off the reservoir, covering the bottom holes as you do so to prevent the fluid draining out.

⚠ Avoid spillages

Brake fluid is highly corrosive, so take care not to spill any on your car bodywork. If you do, wipe it off at once and rinse the affected part with plenty of clean water.

Removing a master cylinder

The master cylinder usually comes off complete with its reservoir, and a new combined cylinder/reservoir is fitted in its place.

Undo the brake pipes leading from the cylinder (**1**), and undo the bolts holding the cylinder to the servo unit (**2**). You can then lift out the cylinder/reservoir and fit a new unit.

If you simply want to get at the servo unit, you may be able to release the master cylinder from the unit with its brake pipes still attached (**3**).

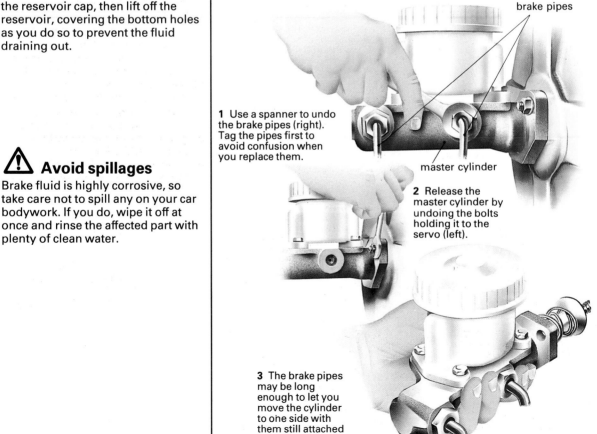

brake pipes

1 Use a spanner to undo the brake pipes (right). Tag the pipes first to avoid confusion when you replace them.

master cylinder

2 Release the master cylinder by undoing the bolts holding it to the servo (left).

3 The brake pipes may be long enough to let you move the cylinder to one side with them still attached (right).

Disconnect pushrod

Before you can take out the old servo to replace it, you have to disconnect the pushrod linking it to the brake pedal. On most cars, the pushrod is linked to the brake pedal by a clevis pin, held in place by a split pin or an R-clip. You may find you have to remove a parcel shelf or trim panel to reach this linkage.

From the driver's foot-well, use pliers to straighten a split pin and then remove it or the R-clip. Then remove the clevis pin by pushing it out sideways.

Unbolt the servo

If you simply wish to replace the servo unit and not the master cylinder, you may be able to move the master cylinder to one side without taking off the brake pipes – they may be long enough to allow you to

Removing a servo unit

Disconnect the master cylinder from the servo unit (**1**). Check the condition of the seal between the two and fit a new one if necessary.

Note how the vacuum hose connects to the servo and then disconnect it by slackening the hose clip (**2**).

Disconnect the pushrod from the brake pedal, then unbolt the servo from the bodywork (**3**). Withdraw the servo (**4**).

1 Undo the bolts holding the master cylinder to the servo and remove the cylinder (above).

servo

2 Disconnect the vacuum hose from the servo by slackening its hose clip (left).

brake pedal

pushrod

bulkhead

rubber gaiter

socket spanner

3 Use a socket spanner to undo the bolts holding the servo to its mounting (above).

4 Withdraw the servo from bulkhead (above).

Uncoupling a pushrod

The pushrod is usually connected to the brake pedal by a clevis pin, held in place by a split pin.

To disconnect the pushrod, straighten out the split pin and pull it out with pliers (below). Then push out the clevis pin.

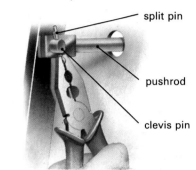

split pin

pushrod

clevis pin

Disconnecting a VW pushrod

On some VWs the pushrod can be pulled straight out of the master cylinder (below); it does not need to be detached from the brake pedal. Check this with your dealer.

When reassembling you may have to adjust the length of the pushrod. To do this, slacken the locknut on the pushrod and turn the rod so that there is about 0.040in (1mm) of free play between the ball end of the rod and its seating in the cylinder piston.

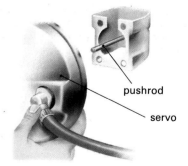

pushrod

servo

Renewing the servo air filter

The air filter is fitted to the back of the servo unit, around the pushrod. On most cars it is made of felt.

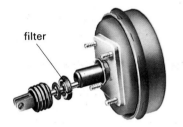

filter

You can reach the filter either from inside the car or by putting your hand in between the back of the servo unit and the bulkhead.

When fitting the new filter, first make a 45° cut across it (see above) so that you can fit it over the pushrod. Once it is in position, press the filter into its recess and cover with the rubber gaiter.

do this.

In this way you do not need to drain the brake fluid out of the system. If you cannot do this, disconnect and remove the master cylinder as described above.

There may be a rubber seal or gasket between the master cylinder and the servo. If so, check its condition and renew it if in doubt.

Make a sketch of the way the vacuum hose is connected to the brake servo, and disconnect it. Find the bolts that secure the servo to the car. They are usually reached from the foot-well inside the car. If they are difficult to reach, use a socket and T-bar. Ask a helper to support the servo while you undo the bolts. Lift the servo clear, working it past the master cylinder. If there is a gasket between the servo unit and the bulkhead, check whether it is worn and renew it if in doubt.

To fit a new servo unit, simply bolt it into place. Reconnect the vacuum hose (after first inspecting it to make sure it's in good condition) and secure it in place with its hose clips. Renew any of these parts if necessary.

When reassembling the pushrod, use a new split pin, not the old one, and be sure to link the rod to the correct hole in the brake pedal – some pedals have more than one.

If you find it difficult to get at the linkage between the pushrod and the brake pedal, try pushing the pin through a piece of adhesive tape, then wrapping the tape around your finger. This will hold the pin in place while you find its hole.

Finally, if the master cylinder has been disconnected, refit it and the

pipes, then bleed the system and top up with fresh brake fluid.

Renew the filter

On most modern cars there is a felt air filter fitted to the rear of the servo unit. It encircles the pushrod.

To renew the filter you do not usually need to take off the servo unit – you should be able to reach the filter from inside the car, or by reaching in between the rear of the unit and the bulkhead. You should change the filter at regular intervals of three years or 36,000 miles (60,000km).

The filter is covered by a rubber gaiter. Undo the clip from the gaiter then slide the gaiter back along the pushrod to expose the filter. Prise the filter out of its recess and pull it off.

Before you fit the new filter, use a sharp knife to slit it across its radius, making the cut at an angle of about 45°. You can now slip the filter easily over the pushrod. Press the two ends of the filter together. Push it into its recess and slide the rubber gaiter on.

On some cars there is a foam-plastic ring instead of a felt ring. This type of filter is not renewable – simply wash it in a weak solution of detergent to remove any dirt, and replace it.

On a few cars the air filter is hidden under a small cover on the outside of the servo. Undo the small central screw holding the cover, lift it off and discard the filter. Fit the new filter and make sure the cover is clean. Fit the cover and tighten up the securing screw.

Single-circuit cylinder

Your car may not have a dual-circuit braking system, in which case your master cylinder will probably look like the one on the right. There is only one pipe leading from the cylinder to the brakes, and you can drain the system from any one bleed nipple.

Removing the cylinder from the brake servo is exactly the same as for a tandem master cylinder. Where the cylinder is fitted without a servo, it is mounted directly on to the bulkhead of the engine compartment.